SKINNY BEEF

MARLYS BIELUNSKI
SUSAN LAMB PARENTI
IRENE YEH, R. D.
of the Meat Board Test Kitchens

Surrey Books
Chicago

SKINNY BEEF is published by Surrey Books, Inc.,
230 E. Ohio St., Suite 120, Chicago, IL 60611.

First edition: 2 3 4 5

This book is manufactured in the United States of America.

Library of Congress Cataloging-in-Publication data:

Bielunski, Marlys.
    Skinny beef / by Marlys Bielunski, Susan Lamb Parenti, Irene Yeh.
    220   p.   cm.
    Includes index.
    ISBN 0-940625-71-7 : $21.95. – ISBN 0-940625-68-7 (pbk.): $12.95
    1. Cookery (Beef) 2. Low-fat diet–Recipes.   3. Low-cholesterol
diet–Recipes.   I. Parenti, Susan Lamb.   II. Yeh, Irene.
III. Title.
RM237.7.B54   1993
641.6'62–dc20   93–4554
                                                                CIP

Art direction: *Hughes & Co., Chicago*
Photography: *Hans Rott, Shigeta Associates, Inc., Chicago*
Food styling: *Lois Hlavac, Judy Vance*
Prop styling: *Nancy Wall Hopkins*
Cover and interior illustrations: *Gwen Connelly, Connelly Design, Inc., Chicago*
Line art illustrations: *Joe Kerr, Chicago*
Nutritional analyses: *Patricia D. Godfrey, C.H.E., R.D., Nutrition & Food
    Associates, Inc., Minneapolis*

The following recipes in this book are adaptations of National Beef Cook-Off®
winners. The contest is sponsored by the American National Cattle Women, Inc., in
cooperation with the Beef Industry Council and Beef Board: Spanish Steak with
Sautéed Vegetables; Harvest-Thyme Beef Sandwiches; Grilled Chopped Steaks with
Corn Relish; Tenderloin Steaks with Pepper Jelly Sauce; Easy Steak Diane.

For free catalog and prices on quantity purchases, contact Surrey Books at the
address above.

This title is distributed to the trade by Publishers Group West.

Other Titles in the "Skinny" Cookbooks Series:

Skinny Cakes, Cookies, and Sweets   *Skinny Potatoes*
Skinny Chocolate   *Skinny Seafood*
Skinny One-Pot Meals   *Skinny Soups*
Skinny Pastas   *Skinny Spices*
Skinny Pizzas

SKINNY BEEF

RICH PLAN®

PREMIUM FOOD PREMIUM SERVICE

a Susie Rich Food Company®

1-800-556-FOOD

Fraser, MI 48026

Dedication

This book is dedicated with appreciation to the farmers and ranchers who produce quality lean beef and to those who enjoy eating it.

Acknowledgments

Special thanks to:

- Peggy Furman, Lisa Janecek, Tonya Parravano, Monica Shetsky, Brenda McDowell, Lisa Piasecki, Suzanne Checchia, Karen Levin, Bonnie Rabert, Mary Sue Peterson, Lee Mooney.

- The Beef Industry Council of the National Live Stock and Meat Board, participating state beef councils, and the Beef Board.

CONTENTS

INTRODUCTION

 Skinny Beef is a book for how you cook and eat today. It's a book that will provide the basics you'll need to create great-tasting meals with beef.

It's packed with information and recipes for the time-pressured person who wants to serve quick, easy, healthful meals for the family—and for entertaining. Whether you're in search of a meal for after work, a fun idea for a Saturday night supper, a quick sandwich or a beef steak on the grill, you'll find everything you need. And *Skinny Beef* is for both the experienced cook and those who need help with the basics. It might be called the guide to "new home cooking."

Here, "new home cooking" means cooking from scratch in the most streamlined ways possible. It's pairing beef with tried-and-true favorites such as soy sauce and ketchup along with newer choices, including salsa and balsamic vinegar. It's also about learning how to use the high-quality prepared foods available in your supermarket in combination with beef and other fresh ingredients to cut time while creating delicious, fresh, healthful meals.

We think you'll appreciate these special features in *Skinny Beef*:

- The introduction to each chapter tells you at a glance what you can expect to find.
- Recipes are easy to prepare—even the classics have been updated and streamlined for today's time-conscious cook. They can be prepared utilizing equipment you already have in your kitchen. Many are one-dish meals incorporating beef with grains, pasta, fruits and vegetables, needing little in the way of extra accompaniments.
- The recipes were created with healthful eating in mind. Fresh ingredients, high-quality prepared food products and low-fat cooking techniques are paired with beef for delicious results.
- Each recipe provides a nutritional analysis, specifying calories, fat, protein, carbohydrate, cholesterol and sodium.
- Step-by-step instructions make it simple even for beginning cooks to prepare and enjoy delicious beef dishes.
- Over 75 recipes can be prepared and cooked in 30 minutes or less. Look for this symbol to quickly identify these recipes.

- Many recipes provide helpful "Cook's Tips" to make preparation even easier.
- Basic information on how to select beef at the grocery store takes the mystery out of buying beef. Beef cooking techniques are explained in detail, so you're assured of delicious results. No more wondering if you're broiling or grilling correctly!
- The latest information on eating for good health is included for your use in meal planning.
- A glossary explains ingredients and cooking terms—some new, some not so new. If you run out of an ingredient, substitutions have been suggested. Equivalent food and measuring yields take the guesswork out of cooking.
- And suggestions for stocking the pantry with ingredients for today's busy cook ensures that what you need will be on hand—when you need it.

This is a book for the 90s' cook. Enjoy!

1.

COOKING FUNDAMENTALS 90s' STYLE

The good news is that lean beef is part of a healthy diet. Today's beef is 27 percent leaner than it was just 20 years ago, thanks to leaner animals and closer trimming of fat at the meat counter.

◆

Healthful Eating–Beef Fits

Today's beef is a "nutritional bargain." This means it has significant amounts of several important nutrients compared to the calories it contains. Beef provides nutrients that are essential for good health such as iron, zinc, protein and five of the B-complex vitamins, including thiamine, niacin, riboflavin, B-6 and B-12.

Health professionals say it's important to eat a variety of foods to get these and other needed nutrients and at the same time not consume too many calories, too much fat, cholesterol, sugar and sodium. Probably the easiest way to ensure that you're getting the variety you should each day is to follow the United States Department of Agriculture (USDA) Food Guide Pyramid.

The Food Guide Pyramid is a general guide, not a rigid rule, to help you make daily food choices. It emphasizes foods from the five major food groups shown below. Each group provides some but not all of the nutrients you need. Foods in one group can't replace those in another. No one food group is more important than another. For good health, you need them all.

Many of the recipes in this book combine beef with ingredients from the other food groups to make a complete meal in one dish.

You'll notice that the Food Guide directly addresses fat in the diet, a health concern for many Americans. If one of your dietary goals is to limit the fat in your daily diet to 30 percent or less of total calories, you can either look at *daily calories from fat* or *maximum grams of fat per day*. For example, a person who consumes 2000 calories can have about 600 fat calories or 67 grams of fat per day.

Tip: Look at your fat intake over the course of a day rather than a single meal.

SUGGESTED DAILY INTAKE OF FAT		
Daily Calorie Level	Daily Calories From Fat	Per Day Maximum Grams of Total Fat
1600	480	53
1800	540	60
2000	**600**	**67**
2200	660	73
2400	720	80
2600	780	87
2800	840	93

Food Guide Pyramid
A Guide to Daily Food Choices

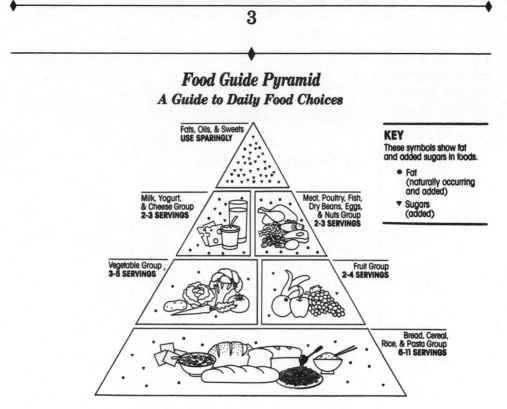

How Many Servings Do You Need Each Day?

	Women & some older adults	Children, teen girls, active women, most men	Teen boys & active men
Calorie level*	about 1,600	about 2,200	about 2,800
Bread group	6	9	11
Vegetable group	3	4	5
Fruit group	2	3	4
Milk group	2-3**	2-3**	2-3**
Meat group	2 for a total of 5 ounces	2 for a total of 6 ounces	3 for a total of 7 ounces

*These are the calorie levels if you choose lowfat, lean foods from the 5 major food groups and use foods from the fats, oils and sweets group sparingly.

**Women who are pregnant or breastfeeding, teenagers, and young adults to age 24 need 3 servings.

Source: U.S. DEPARTMENT OF AGRICULTURE and the
U.S. DEPARTMENT OF HEALTH AND HUMAN SERVICES

Tip: The average 3-ounce cooked, trimmed serving of beef contains about 8.4 grams of fat. Most recipes in this book were designed to provide 3 ounces of cooked, trimmed beef per serving.

3-Ounce Serving

Remember, a serving is defined as 3 ounces of cooked, trimmed meat. Generally, 4 ounces of boneless uncooked beef yields 3 ounces cooked. To visualize, a 3-ounce serving is about the size of a deck of cards or the palm of an average-size woman's hand.

♦ *Nutrition Analysis of Recipes*

Important nutrition information is provided for each recipe in this book. The number of calories; grams of fat, protein and carbohydrate; and milligrams of cholesterol and sodium are shown per individual serving. In addition, the number of calories from fat in the entire recipe as well as from just the beef portion of the recipe are included.

The recipes were analyzed by a registered dietitian of an independent company following these parameters.

- If more than 1 ingredient choice was listed, we used the first option.
- Ingredients listed as optional were not included in the analysis.
- If a range in ingredient amounts was indicated, the lowest amount was used.
- If a range in serving size was indicated, the smallest number of servings was used.
- 90 percent lean ground beef was used for all recipes calling for ground beef.
- If vegetable cooking spray was used to coat a pan, it was not included in the analysis. However, vegetable cooking spray sprayed directly on food was included.

♦ *Lean Cooking Tips*

- Select lean cuts of beef. Look for those with *loin* or *round* in the name.
- Trim fat before cutting beef into strips or cubes for stir-fry or kabobs.

For other cooking methods, cook beef first, then trim any external or inside separable fat before eating.

- Use low-fat cooking methods: broiling; roasting on a rack; panbroiling; grilling; or under cover cookery.
- Use vegetable cooking spray in place of fat for browning meat.
- Cook meats in a heavy nonstick skillet without added fat.
- Reduce oil called for in marinades to no more than 1 teaspoon per ½ cup marinade, or eliminate oil altogether.
- Substitute low-fat, low-calorie versions of ingredients. For example, substitute nonfat plain yogurt for sour cream.
- Cook with fresh ingredients that do not contribute extra fat such as lemon juice, hot and sweet peppers, onion, garlic, tomatoes and ginger.
- To make sauces and gravies lower in calories, reduce the amount of flour or cornstarch used for thickening. Or eliminate the thickening agent altogether. Skim fat from the pan juices, then cook over medium-high heat to thicken as desired.
- Chill soups and stews after cooking in order to remove fat from the surface after it solidifies.
- Stir-fry vegetables in water or broth instead of oil. It not only eliminates a source of fat but the vegetables retain their color better and they're fresher tasting.

Tips on Buying and Storing Beef

With beef selections in the meat case ranging from sirloin steak to ground beef, round tip steaks to top round, tenderloin to tri-tip, you might be confused about what to buy and how to cook it. These tips can help.

◆ Selection

Let the label be your guide. The key is understanding the primal or wholesale cut—it tells you where the meat comes from on the carcass and whether it's a tender cut. For example, the words "loin" and "rib" are clues that the beef is a tender cut. Chuck, round and flank indicate less tender cuts. If the beef cut on the label isn't familiar, ask your meat retailer to explain it.

Inspection ensures that the beef you purchase is of high quality and safe to eat. Federal meat inspection is the responsibility of the Food Safety and Inspection Service (FSIS), a division of the USDA.

Grading is an altogether different process and is optional. Beef can be graded for quality by the USDA. Three grades are usually found at retail: Prime, Choice and Select. Grades are determined by evaluating the amount of marbling (flecks of fat within the lean), the texture of the lean meat and its color and appearance. Meat with the most marbling is labeled Prime. Select has the least amount of fat marbling. It provides fewer calories than Prime or Choice, but it may not be as tender, juicy or flavorful.

When shopping for beef, in addition to reading the label, check for the following:

- Beef should have a bright, cherry-red color, without any grayish or brownish spots. (Vacuum packaged beef may have a darker, purplish-red color because the meat is not in direct contact with the air. When exposed to air, the familiar cherry-red color returns.)
- Make sure beef is firm to the touch rather than soft.
- Choose beef that does not have excess liquid in the package.
- Look for packages that are cold to the touch and not torn or punctured.
- Check the "sell-by" date; purchase only on or before that date.

♦ How Much To Buy

The number of cooked servings you can expect per pound of beef varies according to the beef cut. Boneless cuts yield more servings per pound than cuts with bone. Use the following chart as a guide for determining servings per pound.

Type of Beef	Servings Per Pound (3-ounce cooked, trimmed)
Boneless Cuts (such as top sirloin, top round, ground beef)	3 to 4
Bone-In Cuts (such as chuck arm roast, T-bone steak, rib steak)	2 to 3
Very Bony Cuts (such as ribs)	1 to 1½

♦ Storage

Beef is a perishable food, and proper care must be taken to maintain its quality and safety. The following chart shows how long you can store cooked and uncooked beef in the refrigerator and freezer.

REFRIGERATOR/FREEZER STORAGE TIMETABLE Recommended Storage Times for Maximum Quality		
Type of Beef	Refrigerator (36°F to 40°F)	Freezer (0°F or Colder)
Beef Steaks, Roasts	3 to 4 days	6 to 12 months
Ground Beef	1 to 2 days	3 to 4 months
Leftover Cooked Beef	3 to 4 days	2 to 3 months

♦ Keep It Safe—Food Handling Tips

Most food-related illnesses are caused by microorganisms, parasites and viruses that are all around us—in the air and soil, on our skin, and in raw or undercooked foods. Most can be controlled by proper food handling both in the marketplace and at home. It's your responsibility to keep food safe to eat after it has been purchased, brought home and stored or cooked.

- Refrigerate or freeze meat as soon as you get home from a shopping trip.
- The safest way to defrost meat is to take it out of the freezer and place it in the refrigerator overnight. Never defrost frozen meat on the kitchen counter.
- It's not necessary to bring meat to room temperature before cooking. Recipes in this book are based on meat taken directly from the refrigerator.
- Promptly and properly store meats, sauces, gravies and perishable foods after the meal is over. Don't cool leftovers on the kitchen counter. Wrap and refrigerate or freeze meat in portions you'll use at one time. Divide large portions into smaller portions for faster cooling and less chance of bacterial growth.
- To guard against cross-contamination of food products, thoroughly clean your hands, cutting surface and knife after coming in contact with raw meat or poultry.
- Boards used for chopping and other meat and food preparations should be washed in hot soapy water after each use. Carving boards should be used exclusively for carving.
- Do not eat raw meat.
- The USDA recommends cooking ground beef at least to medium (160°F) doneness or until the juices run clear and the center is no longer pink; other cuts can be cooked as desired, rare to well-done. The reason that ground beef should be cooked at least to medium doneness is that it's more susceptible to bacteria; grinding meat can transfer surface bacteria to the interior of the ground meat.

Beef Cookery

The secret to moist, juicy, flavorful beef is in the cooking, but not all beef cuts can be cooked in the same way. The chart on page 8 highlights the beef cuts used in this book and the most appropriate cooking methods for them.

♦ Cooking Methods

A variety of cooking methods can be used to prepare beef. The most commonly used ones are described here.

Broiling Broiling is a low-fat cooking method for steaks, ground beef patties and other tender cuts of meat. Less tender beef cuts, such as flank or top round steak, should be marinated before broiling. Thinner cuts (¾ to 1 inch thick) should be positioned 2 to 3 inches from the heat; thicker cuts, 3 to 6 inches. Place meat on a rack in the broiler pan so fat can drip away during cooking.

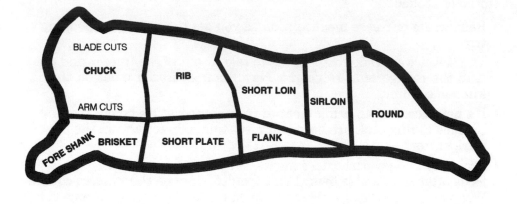

BEEF CUT	HOW TO COOK				
	Stir-Fry/ Sauté	Panbroil	Broil	Grill	Under Cover Cooking
SHORT LOIN T-Bone Steak, Porterhouse Steak		X	X	X	
Tenderloin Steak (Filet)	X	X	X	X	
Tenderloin Roast			X	X	X
Top Loin (Strip) Steak, Boneless	X	X	X	X	
ROUND Tip Steak, Thin Cut	X	X			
Round Steak					X
Top Round Steak	X*	X*	X*	X*	X
Eye Round Roast				X*	X
Eye Round Steak		X*	X*	X*	
RIB Rib Steak, Rib Eye Steak	X	X	X	X	
CHUCK Top Blade Steak, Boneless	X	X	X	X	X
Shoulder Pot Roast, Steak, Boneless					X
Arm, Blade, 7-Bone Pot Roast					X
SIRLOIN Sirloin Steak, Flat Bone, Round Bone	X	X	X	X	
Top Sirloin Steak, Boneless	X	X	X	X	
Tri-Tip Roast (Bottom Sirloin)			X	X	
FLANK Flank Steak	X		X*	X*	X
OTHER CUTS Ground Beef	X	X	X	X	
Cubed Steak	X	X			X
Beef For Stew					X
Cubes For Kabobs			X	X	

*Generally marinate 6 hours or as long as overnight prior to cooking.

Panbroiling   Sometimes described as "frying without fat," panbroiling is a quick and easy, low-fat, stove top cooking method for cooking ground beef patties and steaks that are 1 inch thick or less. The difference between broiling and panbroiling is that for broiling the heat source is from the top; for panbroiling it is underneath the pan. Beef is placed in a preheated heavy nonstick skillet and cooked uncovered over medium to medium-low heat, turning once. Fat should be removed as it accumulates.

Sautéing   Sautéing is a quick cooking method, sometimes called panfrying, for tender beef cuts such as steaks and ground beef patties. It's similar to panbroiling except that a small amount of oil is added to the pan. Cooking is done uncovered over medium heat, and the beef is turned occasionally.

Stir-Frying   This is a fast way of cooking uniform size pieces of beef with vegetables and other ingredients. It's a variation of sautéing that is done in a wok or large, heavy skillet, uncovered, over medium to medium-high heat. Beef should be cooked in batches, if necessary, to prevent overcrowding. Overcrowding can cause meat to steam. Meat and other ingredients must be continuously turned with a scooping motion to ensure even cooking.

Grilling   Grilling is a low-fat method of cooking steaks, burgers and kabobs about 4 to 5 inches directly above coals so that the heat source is underneath the food—the opposite of broiling. Meat is generally turned once during grilling. The grill may be open or covered; coals should be at medium temperature to ensure even cooking. (For gas grills, consult manufacturer's directions as cooking methods, times and temperatures may be different from charcoal grilling.)

Roasting   Roasting is a simple low-fat cooking method for roasts and thicker steaks (2 inches thick or more). Roasting requires little attention and only three pieces of equipment: a shallow roasting pan with rack and a meat thermometer. Meat is placed on a rack in the roasting pan, without water, and the meat thermometer is inserted into the thickest part, not touching bone or fat. Roasts should be removed from the oven when the thermometer reads 5 to 10 degrees below desired doneness, as the temperature will rise during standing.

Under Cover Cooking   Moist heat cookery, or "under cover cooking," uses the steam from simmering liquid to cook meat. It is important to simmer rather than boil (the high temperature needed to boil can toughen meat) and use a pan with a tight-fitting lid. There are three types of under cover cooking: (1) *braising*—meat is browned then simmered in a small amount of liquid; (2) *cooking in liquid*—meat is simmered in just enough liquid to cover it; and (3) *poaching*—a roast is first browned, then simmered in liquid to cover.

Braising and cooking in liquid are used for cooking less tender beef cuts to fork tenderness. Poaching is suitable for tender roasts such as tenderloin or rib eye and less tender cuts such as eye round.

Cook's Tip: Do not use a fork for turning beef during cooking. It can pierce the meat, allowing flavorful juices to escape.

♦ About Marinades

Marinades are highly seasoned liquids such as fruit or vegetable juices, wine, water and oil combined with herbs and seasonings that add flavor and, in some cases, tenderize beef.

To tenderize, a marinade must contain an acidic ingredient such as lemon juice, wine, vinegar or yogurt. The acid penetrates meat fibers and helps tenderize them, but only to about ¼ inch from the cut surface. For tenderization, most cuts need to be marinated at least 6 hours or as long as overnight. Marinating longer than 24 hours can break down meat fibers and cause a mushy texture.

When marinating for flavor, beef should be covered with the marinade for 15 minutes to 2 hours. Allow a little longer marinating time for a roast or thick steak (more than 1 inch thick).

Beef should always be marinated in the refrigerator. If the marinade is to be used later for basting or as a sauce, a portion of the marinade should be reserved for that purpose prior to adding the beef.

Allow about ¼ to ½ cup of marinade for each 1 to 2 pounds of beef. A heavy-duty plastic food-safe bag is convenient for marinating. A glass dish may also be used. Turn beef occasionally during marinating so all sides are equally exposed to the marinade.

A dry flavor marinade, or rub, is a mixture of crushed herbs, spices and sometimes salt that is rubbed onto the surface of steaks and roasts prior to cooking. Dry flavor marinades will not tenderize the meat.

♦ Determining Doneness

How can you tell if beef is cooked to the doneness you prefer? There are several ways, depending upon the cut.

For steaks and other thin cuts that are broiled, panbroiled or grilled, the easiest way to determine doneness is by cutting a small slit and checking the color of the meat near the bone, or near the center of a boneless cut.

VISUAL GUIDE TO DETERMINING DONENESS OF STEAKS AND ROASTS

Rare—Center is bright red; pinkish toward outer portion.

Medium—Center is light pink; outer portion is brown.

Well-done—Uniform brown throughout.

For roasts and thicker steaks (2 inches thick or more), a meat thermometer is the quickest way to determine doneness. Two types of thermometers can be used: (1) a meat thermometer, which is inserted into the roast prior to cooking and left in the roast during the entire cooking process, or (2) an instant-read thermometer inserted for about 10 seconds, then removed. An instant-read thermometer is not oven safe. Use it toward the end of the minimum cooking time.

The following chart shows the recommended temperatures.

RECOMMENDED INTERNAL TEMPERATURE FOR BEEF	
Rare	140°F
Medium-rare	150°F
Medium	160°F
Well-done	170°F
Ground beef	160°F–170°F

2.
KITCHEN HELPS

S ometimes we all need help in the kitchen. Whether it's what size pan to use, how many teaspoons equal a tablespoon or what to do if you've run out of honey mustard, this section of the book can provide answers and solutions.

Equivalents—How Much Do You Need?

How many fresh lemons does it take to make ½ cup of juice, or how many slices of bread does it take to make a cup of crumbs? There's no more guesswork with the following handy chart. Use it as a guide, keeping in mind that amounts are approximate.

♦ *Equivalent Yields*

Fruits
1 medium lemon = 3 tablespoons juice, 2 teaspoons grated peel
1 medium lime = 1 to 2 tablespoons juice, 1½ to 2 teaspoons grated peel
1 medium orange = ¼ cup juice, 2 teaspoons grated peel
1 large apple = 1 cup sliced apple
1 pound apples = 3 medium apples

Pastas, Noodles, Rice
8 ounces uncooked elbow macaroni = 4 cups cooked macaroni
8 ounces uncooked medium width noodles = 3¾ cups cooked noodles
8 ounces uncooked spaghetti = 4 cups cooked spaghetti
1 cup uncooked regular long grain rice = 3 cups cooked rice
1 cup uncooked enriched instant rice = 2 cups cooked rice
1 cup uncooked brown rice = 3 to 4 cups cooked rice

Vegetables
1 small head cabbage (1 pound) = 4 to 4½ cups shredded cabbage
1 large carrot = 1 cup shredded carrot
2 medium celery stalks = 1 cup diced or chopped celery
1 large green bell pepper = 1 cup diced green bell pepper
1 medium head lettuce = 6 cups torn lettuce
¾ pound raw mushrooms = 3 cups sliced raw mushrooms
1 medium onion = ½ cup chopped onion
1 pound all-purpose potatoes = 3 medium potatoes
1 pound tomatoes = 2 large, 3 medium or 4 small tomatoes

Miscellaneous
1 small garlic clove = ½ teaspoon minced or crushed garlic
1 cup beef broth = 1 bouillon cube or 1 teaspoon bouillon granules
    dissolved in 1 cup boiling water
1 teaspoon dried herbs = 1 tablespoon chopped fresh herbs
1½ slices bread = 1 cup soft bread crumbs
4 ounces firm cheese (Cheddar, Monterey Jack, Swiss) = 1 cup
    shredded cheese
3 to 4 ounces hard cheese (Parmesan, Romano) = approximately ½ cup
    grated cheese
¼ pound (1 stick) butter or margarine = ½ cup = 8 tablespoons

---

Successful Measuring

Successful recipe results depend on exact measurements. These tips will help you measure exactly.

• Measure flour, sugar and other dry or solid ingredients in graduated measuring cups (usually metal or plastic cups in sets that include 1-cup, ½-cup, ⅓-cup and ¼-cup measures) that can be filled to the top and leveled with a spatula or the flat side of a table knife. Don't shake or pack dry ingredients unless specified in the recipe (example: packed brown sugar should be pressed firmly into the cup).

- Measure liquid ingredients in clear glass (or plastic) measuring cups with a spout. Place cup on a level surface and add desired amount of liquid; read the measure at eye level.

- Measure small amounts of both dry and liquid ingredients in measuring spoons.

MEASURING EQUIVALENTS	
Dash or pinch	under ⅛ teaspoon
½ tablespoon	1½ teaspoons
1 tablespoon	3 teaspoons
1 ounce liquid	2 tablespoons
¼ cup	4 tablespoons
⅓ cup	5 tablespoons, plus 1 teaspoon
½ cup	8 tablespoons
⅔ cup	10 tablespoons, plus 2 teaspoons
¾ cup	12 tablespoons
1 cup	16 tablespoons
1 cup	8 ounces
1 pound	16 ounces

Kitchen Equipment

Recipes in this book use basic cooking equipment such as skillets, Dutch ovens, saucepans, broiler pan with rack and muffin tins. For best results, always use the type and size of pan specified in the recipe. Cookware that is too large can cause overcooking. A pan that is too small can cause spillovers. When in doubt, the following charts can serve as guidelines for selecting the correct size.

Casserole Size	Baking Dish Substitution
1½-quart	10 × 6-inch
2-quart	11 × 7-inch or 8-inch square
2½-quart	9-inch square
3-quart	13 × 9-inch

Saucepan Size	Saucepan Volume
Small	1 to 1½ quarts (4 to 6 cups)
Medium	2 quarts (8 cups)
Large	3 to 4 quarts (12 to 16 cups)
Dutch Oven/ Stock Pot	5 to 8 quarts (20 to 32 cups)

Skillet Size	Skillet Diameter
Small	6 to 8 inches
Medium	8 to 10 inches
Large	10 to 12 inches

Substitutions

What can you do if you run out of an ingredient? What are suitable substitutions? This chart can help.

For	Substitute
1 tablespoon balsamic vinegar	1 tablespoon red wine vinegar *plus* ½ teaspoon sugar
olive oil	equal amount of vegetable oil (olive oil does have a more pronounced flavor)
roasted red peppers (jarred)	equal amount pimientos
⅓ cup honey mustard	⅓ cup Dijon-style mustard *plus* 1½ tablespoons honey
whole milk	equal amount 2%, 1% or skim milk
sour cream	equal amount plain low-fat or nonfat yogurt; reduced-calorie or nonfat sour cream product
1 tablespoon chopped fresh herbs	1 teaspoon dried herbs
1 teaspoon grated fresh ginger	¼ teaspoon ground ginger
1 cup ready-to-serve beef broth	1 bouillon cube or 1 teaspoon instant bouillon granules *plus* 1 cup boiling water
beef consommé	equal amount condensed beef broth
½ teaspoon minced garlic (1 small clove)	½ teaspoon jarred garlic or ⅛ teaspoon garlic powder
cilantro	equal amount parsley (for color; the flavor of fresh cilantro cannot be duplicated)

The 90s' Pantry

A well-stocked pantry makes meal preparation easier. Replenish supplies before they're depleted so you won't be caught short.

♦ *Lower-Fat Ingredients*

- low-fat/reduced-fat/nonfat salad dressings
- reduced-calorie/nonfat mayonnaise
- canned or jarred low-fat spaghetti sauce
- vegetable cooking spray

♦ *Basics*

- all-purpose flour
- salt and pepper
- cornmeal
- cornstarch
- vegetable oil
- brown sugar
- honey
- jellies, jams, preserves
- ketchup
- barbecue sauce
- peanut butter
- canned whole peeled tomatoes
- canned tomato sauce, tomato paste
- jarred pimiento
- canned peaches, pineapple chunks
- canned cranberry sauce
- soy sauce
- canned ready-to-serve beef broth
- instant bouillon granules, cubes
- pastas—spaghetti, macaroni
- rices—regular long grain, brown

♦ *Timesaving Ingredients*

- recipe-ready tomatoes (canned diced tomatoes with Italian or Mexican seasonings)
- canned or jarred pasta sauces
- jarred brown gravy
- jarred roasted red bell peppers
- canned green chilies
- canned beans—black, pinto, chili, kidney
- canned or jarred vegetable juice
- instant rice
- ramen noodles
- bread crumbs
- corn muffin mix
- dried minced onions
- jarred garlic
- garlic powder
- prepared seasoning mixes (Italian, lemon pepper, garlic pepper)

♦ *Ingredients That Add Variety*

- vinegars—balsamic, rice, red wine, white wine, cider
- spices/seasonings—curry, basil, oregano, rosemary, red pepper (cayenne), thyme, cumin, chili powder, paprika, ginger, cinnamon, sesame seed
- mustards—Dijon, coarse-grain, honey
- Major Grey chutney
- hoisin sauce
- teriyaki sauce
- salsa, picante sauce
- hot pepper sauce
- oils—olive, Oriental dark sesame
- pastas—vermicelli, lasagna, bow ties, spirals
- quick-cooking barley
- couscous
- lentils
- tortillas—corn, flour
- pita bread
- artichoke hearts—canned plain, marinated
- nuts
- raisins

3.
QUICK MAIN DISH SALADS

 ain dish salads are mainstays for the "quick cook." The versatile array in this chapter includes both warm and chilled choices, pairing beef with fresh vegetables and fruits, pastas and grains.

Salad making is especially easy these days when you take advantage of the ready-to-use produce in the supermarket. Salad bars offer many basic fruits and vegetables, cleaned, trimmed and, in some cases, cut into bite-size pieces. Also, look for bags of pre-washed spinach and mixed salad greens, cabbage already shredded for coleslaw and recipe-ready broccoli, carrots, celery and cauliflower florets.

For the utmost convenience, lean deli roast beef can be used in several of these recipes. In others, beef is quickly stir-fried, grilled or broiled. (*Smart cook's tip*: Plan ahead when you grill or broil. Cook an extra steak to use in a different salad a night or two later.)

BEEF GAZPACHO SALAD

The flavors of spicy, tomato-based gazpacho are prominent in this quick and easy salad made with deli roast beef. The beef is already cooked, ready to serve. Just order the amount you need, sliced to order. Pick up the veggies ready-to-use from the salad bar.

Preparation time: 20 minutes
Chilling time: 1 hour

- ¾ pound deli roast beef, sliced ¼ inch thick
- 4 cups torn mixed salad greens
- 1 cup sliced cucumber
- 1 small avocado, cut into 8 wedges (optional)

Gazpacho Dressing

- 1 can (5½ ounces) spicy hot 100% vegetable juice
- ½ cup chopped tomato
- ¼ cup finely chopped green bell pepper
- 1 tablespoon red wine vinegar
- 1 tablespoon chopped fresh cilantro (optional)
- 2 teaspoons olive oil
- 1 clove garlic, crushed

1. Trim fat from deli roast beef. Stack beef slices; cut lengthwise in half and then crosswise into ½-inch wide strips. In large bowl, combine dressing ingredients. Add beef; toss to coat. Cover and refrigerate at least 1 hour.

2. To serve, arrange salad greens on serving platter; arrange cucumber and avocado, if desired, around outside edge. Spoon beef mixture onto center of salad greens.

Cook's Tip: Three-quarters pound leftover cooked beef steak or roast, sliced ¼ inch thick and cut into 1½-inch wide strips, may be substituted for deli roast beef.

Makes 4 servings (serving size: 2 cups).

Nutritional Information Per Serving

Calories:	206	Protein (g):	26
Calories from total fat: 76		Carbohydrate (g):	6
(Calories from fat in beef: 53)		Cholesterol (mg):	69
Fat (g):	8	Sodium (mg):	214

STIR-FRIED BEEF & GREENS

This salad of stir-fried beef, colorful veggies and warm balsamic vinaigrette tops mixed greens. Add crusty whole grain rolls for a complete, quick meal.

Total preparation and cooking time: 25 minutes

1–pound beef top round **or** boneless top sirloin steak, cut ¾ inch thick **or** flank steak

4 cups torn mixed spinach leaves and leaf lettuce

1 cup frozen corn, defrosted

½ to 1 cup thinly sliced red onion

½ cup jarred roasted red pepper strips

3 tablespoons balsamic vinegar

Marinade

3 tablespoons olive oil

2 tablespoons balsamic vinegar

2 cloves garlic, crushed

¾ teaspoon salt

¾ teaspoon dried thyme leaves

¼ teaspoon pepper

1. Trim fat from beef steak. Cut steak lengthwise in half and then crosswise into ⅛-inch thick strips. In medium bowl, whisk together marinade ingredients. Add beef; toss to coat. Set aside.

2. Arrange salad greens on serving platter.

3. Remove beef from marinade; reserve marinade. Heat large nonstick skillet over medium-high heat until hot. Add beef (half at a time) and stir-fry 1 minute or until outside surface is no longer pink. (Do not overcook.) Add corn, onion and red pepper to beef and continue cooking 30 seconds. Spoon onto salad greens.

4. In same skillet, add reserved marinade and 3 tablespoons balsamic vinegar; bring to a boil. Spoon over salad and serve immediately.

Makes 4 servings (serving size: 2 cups).

Nutritional Information Per Serving

Calories:	306	Protein (g):	30
Calories from total fat: 134		Carbohydrate (g):	15
(Calories from fat in beef: 38)		Cholesterol (mg):	71
Fat (g):	15	Sodium (mg):	479

Step 1. **Trim fat from steak.**

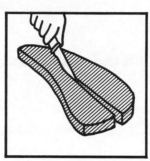

Step 2. **Cut steak lengthwise in half.**

Step 3. **Cut crosswise into thin strips.**

CITRUSY BEEF & VEGETABLE COUSCOUS SALAD

Bring a taste of the Mediterranean to your table. Cinnamon-laced couscous studded with raisins is combined with cucumber, carrots, stir-fried strips of sirloin and an orange vinaigrette for a cool, refreshing one-dish meal.

Total preparation and cooking time: 30 minutes
Chilling time: 6 to 8 hours or overnight, if desired

1–pound	boneless beef top sirloin steak, cut 1 inch thick
1½ cups	water
1 cup	couscous
⅓ cup	golden raisins
½ teaspoon	ground cinnamon
½ teaspoon	salt
1 tablespoon	olive oil
2 cloves	garlic, crushed
⅛ teaspoon	ground red pepper
1 cup	chopped cucumber
½ cup	shredded carrot
½ teaspoon	salt
3 tablespoons	frozen orange juice concentrate, defrosted
1 tablespoon	cider vinegar
	Romaine lettuce leaves

1. Bring water to a boil. Add couscous, raisins, cinnamon and ½ teaspoon salt; remove from heat. Let stand covered 5 minutes; uncover and stir with fork to fluff. Cool.

2. Meanwhile trim fat from beef steak. Cut steak lengthwise in half and then crosswise into ¼-inch thick strips. In medium bowl, combine oil, garlic and red pepper. Add beef; toss to coat.

3. In large bowl, combine couscous mixture, cucumber and carrot; mix lightly. Set aside.

4. Heat large nonstick skillet over medium-high heat until hot. Add beef (half at a time) and stir-fry 1 to 2 minutes or until outside surface is no longer pink. Remove beef from skillet with slotted spoon; season

with ½ teaspoon salt. In same skillet, add orange juice concentrate and vinegar; cook and stir until reduced and slightly thickened. Remove from heat; add beef and toss to coat. Add to couscous mixture, mixing lightly. Cover and refrigerate 6 to 8 hours or overnight, if desired.

5. To serve, arrange lettuce on serving platter; top with beef and couscous mixture.

Makes 4 servings (serving size: 1½ cups).

Nutritional Information Per Serving

Calories:	427	Protein (g):	34
Calories from total fat: 90		Carbohydrate (g):	50
(Calories from fat in beef: 55)		Cholesterol (mg):	76
Fat (g):	10	Sodium (mg):	605

BEEF, TOMATO & BASIL SALAD WITH GARLIC CROUTONS

A great make-ahead salad! Prepare all the fixings in advance—the croutons, veggies and dressing—then toss with strips of stir-fried beef at serving time. (See photograph)

Total preparation and cooking time: 35 minutes

1–pound boneless beef top sirloin steak **or** top loin steaks, cut 1 inch thick
3 tablespoons olive oil
2 large cloves garlic, crushed
3 slices (1 inch thick) firm Italian **or** sourdough bread
2 tablespoons balsamic vinegar
¼ teaspoon sugar
¼ teaspoon pepper
2 ripe medium tomatoes, cut into ¾-inch pieces
1 medium yellow bell pepper, cut into ½-inch pieces
½ small red onion, thinly sliced
½ cup thinly sliced fresh basil, lightly packed
Vegetable cooking spray
½ teaspoon salt
Lettuce leaves

1. Heat oven to 400°. In 1-cup glass measure, heat oil and garlic in microwave at high 45 seconds; cool. Lightly brush bread slices with 1 tablespoon oil mixture; cut into 1-inch cubes. Place on baking sheet. Bake in 400° oven 8 to 10 minutes or until crisp and golden brown; cool.

2. In large bowl, whisk together remaining 2 tablespoons oil mixture, vinegar, sugar and pepper. Add tomatoes, bell pepper, onion and basil; toss to coat. Cover and refrigerate. (Vegetable mixture can be made ahead and refrigerated up to 24 hours.)

3. Meanwhile trim fat from beef steak. Cut steak lengthwise in half and then crosswise into ½-inch thick strips. Spray large nonstick skillet with cooking spray. Heat skillet over medium-high heat until hot. Add beef and stir-fry 3 minutes or until outside surface is no longer pink. Season with salt.

4. To serve, arrange lettuce on serving platter. Add croutons and beef to vegetable mixture; mix lightly. Spoon beef mixture onto lettuce. Serve immediately.

Makes 6 servings (serving size: about 1 cup).

Nutritional Information Per Serving

Calories:	229	Protein (g):	19
Calories from total fat: 101		Carbohydrate (g):	13
(Calories from fat in beef: 55)		Cholesterol (mg):	51
Fat (g):	11	Sodium (mg):	303

ASIAN BEEF SALAD

A delicious blend of Oriental flavors stars in the dressing for this broiled sirloin salad. For a quicker version, use deli roast beef and eliminate the cooking. (See photograph)

Total preparation and cooking time: 30 minutes

- 1–pound boneless beef top sirloin steak, cut 1 inch thick
- ½ medium red onion, cut into thin wedges
- 3 tablespoons chopped fresh cilantro
- 4 cups torn mixed salad greens **or** thinly sliced nappa cabbage
- 2 tablespoons coarsely chopped peanuts (optional)

Citrus-Soy Dressing
- 2 tablespoons fresh lime juice
- 2 tablespoons soy sauce
- 1 tablespoon sugar
- 2 teaspoons dark sesame oil
- 1 green serrano chili pepper, seeded, finely chopped
- 1 large clove garlic, crushed

1. Place beef steak on rack in broiler pan so surface of meat is 3 to 4 inches from heat. Broil 16 to 18 minutes for rare to medium doneness, turning once. Let stand 10 minutes. Trim fat from steak. Carve steak crosswise into slices.

2. In medium bowl, combine beef, onion and cilantro.

3. In small bowl, whisk together dressing ingredients. Pour over beef mixture; toss to coat.

4. Arrange salad greens on serving platter; top with beef mixture. Sprinkle with peanuts, if desired. Serve immediately.

Cook's Tip: Three-quarters pound deli roast beef, sliced ¼ inch thick and cut into 1-inch wide strips, may be substituted for beef top sirloin steak.

Makes 4 servings (serving size: 2 cups).

Nutritional Information Per Serving

Calories:	226	Protein (g):	28
Calories from total fat: 78		Carbohydrate (g):	9
(Calories from fat in beef: 55)		Cholesterol (mg):	76
Fat (g):	9	Sodium (mg):	597

GREEK BEEF SALAD

Favorite Greek flavors star in this entree salad that's served with toasted pita bread. Preparation is easy—while the steak broils, there's ample time to prepare the remaining salad ingredients. (See photograph)

Total preparation and cooking time: 30 minutes

- 1–pound beef top round steak, cut 1 inch thick
- 6 cups torn romaine lettuce
- 1 medium cucumber, cut lengthwise in half and thinly sliced
- ½ small red onion, cut into thin wedges
- 2 tablespoons crumbled feta cheese
- 8 Greek **or** ripe olives (optional)
- 2 whole pita pocket breads, cut in half

Lemon-Oregano Dressing
- 5 tablespoons fresh lemon juice
- 3 tablespoons olive oil
- 1 teaspoon dried oregano leaves
- ½ teaspoon salt
- ¼ teaspoon pepper

1. Place beef steak on rack in broiler pan so surface of meat is 3 to 4 inches from heat. Broil 15 to 18 minutes for rare to medium doneness, turning once. Let stand 10 minutes. Trim fat from steak. Carve steak crosswise into thin slices.

2. Meanwhile in large bowl, whisk together dressing ingredients. Add beef, lettuce, cucumber and onion; toss to coat. Sprinkle with cheese. Garnish with olives, if desired.

3. Toast pita bread halves in toaster until warm; cut each half into thirds. Serve with salad.

Cook's Tip: Three-quarters pound deli roast beef, sliced ¼ inch thick and cut into 1-inch wide strips, may be substituted for beef top round steak.

Makes 4 servings (serving size: 2 cups).

Nutritional Information Per Serving

Calories:	396	Protein (g):	34
Calories from total fat: 145		Carbohydrate (g):	29
(Calories from fat in beef: 38)		Cholesterol (mg):	75
Fat (g):	16	Sodium (mg):	580

Warm Cabbage, Apple & Beef Sausage Salad

Reminiscent of a long-simmering recipe, this one is 30-minutes-quick. Fully-cooked sausage that needs only to be heated through prior to serving is paired with pre-shredded coleslaw mix, apple wedges and a piquant mustard sauce spiked with apple jelly.

Total preparation and cooking time: 30 minutes

- ½–pound reduced-fat fully-cooked smoked beef sausage link, cut into ½-inch thick slices
- 2 teaspoons vegetable oil
- 1 small onion, cut into thin wedges
- 2 medium red apples, each cut into 12 wedges
- 6½ cups (¾ pound) packaged coleslaw mix
- ½ teaspoon salt (optional)

Dressing
- ¼ cup apple jelly
- 2 tablespoons cider vinegar
- 1 tablespoon Dijon-style mustard
- ¼ teaspoon pepper

1. In large nonstick skillet, heat oil over medium heat until hot. Add onion and apples; cover and cook 5 minutes. Stir in coleslaw mix; continue cooking, covered, 2 to 4 minutes or until cabbage is crisp-tender. Season with salt, if desired. Remove to serving platter; keep warm.

2. In same skillet, add beef sausage; cook and stir over medium-high heat 2 minutes. Stir in combined dressing ingredients; cook 2 minutes or until sauce is reduced and slightly thickened. Spoon over cabbage mixture. Serve immediately.

Cook's Tip: The shredded cabbage in the packaged coleslaw mix may vary in thickness. Watch cooking time carefully; do not overcook. Thinly sliced green cabbage may be substituted for packaged coleslaw mix.

Makes 4 servings (serving size: 2 cups).

Nutritional Information Per Serving

Calories:	274	Protein (g):	10
Calories from total fat: 125		Carbohydrate (g):	32
(Calories from fat in beef: 99)		Cholesterol (mg):	36
Fat (g):	14	Sodium (mg):	580

Beef, Pasta & Artichoke Toss with Balsamic Vinaigrette

A hearty salad, special enough for company, perfect for "toting" to picnics or bring-a-dish suppers. Most of the ingredients are probably in your pantry right now! And it can be made the night before if time is short.

Total preparation and cooking time: 30 minutes
Chilling time: 2 hours or overnight, if desired

1½–pound boneless beef sirloin steak, cut
    1 inch thick
4 cups uncooked tri-colored rotelle
    (spiral-shaped) pasta
1 can (14 ounces) quartered artichoke hearts,
    drained
1 large red bell pepper, cut into julienne strips
1 cup small pitted ripe olives (optional)
2 tablespoons thinly sliced fresh basil

Balsamic Vinaigrette
¼ cup olive oil
¼ cup balsamic vinegar
1½ teaspoons dried basil leaves
¾ teaspoon salt
¼ teaspoon pepper

1. Place beef steak on rack in broiler pan so surface of meat is 3 to 4 inches from heat. Broil steak 16 to 18 minutes for rare to medium doneness, turning once. Let stand 10 minutes. Trim fat from steak. Cut steak lengthwise in half and then crosswise into thin slices.

2. Meanwhile cook pasta according to package directions. Drain; rinse with cold water.

3. In large bowl, combine beef, pasta, artichoke hearts, bell pepper, olives, if desired, and fresh basil; mix lightly.

4. In small bowl, whisk together vinaigrette ingredients. Pour over beef mixture; toss to coat. Cover and refrigerate at least 2 hours or overnight, if desired, before serving.

Cook's Tip: One pound deli roast beef, sliced ¼ inch thick and cut into 1-inch wide strips, may be substituted for beef sirloin steak.

Makes 8 servings (serving size: 1½ cups).

Nutritional Information Per Serving

Calories:	331	Protein (g):	25
Calories from total fat: 108		Carbohydrate (g):	30
(Calories from fat in beef: 41)		Cholesterol (mg):	57
Fat (g):	12	Sodium (mg):	274

COLORFUL TACO SALAD

Taco salad was never so easy! Homemade Spicy Seasoning Mix adds just the right Tex-Mex flavors to ground beef and onion. Simmer just 10 minutes and serve atop lettuce with chopped yellow bell pepper, sliced green onions and tortilla chips.

Total preparation and cooking time: 30 minutes

- 1 pound lean ground beef
- 1 medium onion, chopped
- 1 tablespoon Spicy Seasoning Mix (recipe follows)
- ½ teaspoon salt
- 1 can (14½ ounces) Mexican-style diced tomatoes, undrained
- 4 to 6 cups torn lettuce leaves
  Chopped yellow bell pepper, sliced green onions and tortilla chips (optional)

1. In large nonstick skillet, brown ground beef and onion over medium heat 8 to 10 minutes or until beef is no longer pink, breaking up into ¾-inch crumbles. Pour off drippings.

2. Sprinkle seasoning mix and salt over beef. Stir in tomatoes; simmer 10 minutes, stirring occasionally.

3. Meanwhile place lettuce on 4 individual plates; top each with ¼ of beef mixture. Sprinkle with bell pepper and green onions, if desired. Garnish with tortilla chips, if desired.

Makes 4 servings (serving size: ¼ of recipe).

Nutritional Information Per Serving

Calories:	223	Protein (g):	24
Calories from total fat: 88		Carbohydrate (g):	12
(Calories from fat in beef: 82)		Cholesterol (mg):	70
Fat (g):	10	Sodium (mg):	535

SPICY SEASONING MIX

Preparation time: 5 minutes

3 tablespoons chili powder
2 teaspoons ground cumin
1½ teaspoons garlic powder
¾ teaspoon dried oregano leaves
½ teaspoon ground red pepper

1. Combine all ingredients. Cover and store in airtight container. Shake before using to blend.

Makes about ⅓ cup.

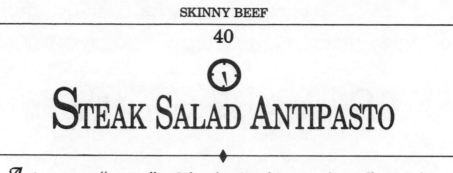

STEAK SALAD ANTIPASTO

Antipasto means "appetizer" in Italian, but this salad is a meal in itself, with Italian bread as an accompaniment. Serve cappuccino and biscotti (Italian cookies) for dessert.

Total preparation and cooking time: 30 minutes

- 1–pound boneless beef top sirloin steak, cut 1 inch thick
- 1 jar (6 ounces) marinated artichoke hearts
- ⅓ cup prepared fat-free Italian dressing
- 2 tablespoons thinly sliced fresh basil
- 3 ounces part-skim mozzarella cheese, cut into ½-inch cubes
- 2 plum tomatoes, each cut into 6 wedges
- ¼ cup kalamata **or** ripe olives (optional)
- 4 cups torn romaine lettuce

1. Place beef steak on rack in broiler pan so surface of meat is 3 to 4 inches from heat. Broil 16 to 18 minutes for rare to medium doneness, turning once. Let stand 10 minutes.

2. Meanwhile drain artichoke hearts, reserving marinade in small bowl. Add Italian dressing and basil to marinade, stirring to blend.

3. In medium bowl, combine artichoke hearts, cheese, tomatoes, olives, if desired, and 2 tablespoons dressing mixture; toss lightly. (Can be prepared a day ahead, if desired. Cover and refrigerate.)

4. Arrange lettuce on serving platter. Trim fat from steak. Carve steak crosswise into slices; place on lettuce down center of platter. Arrange vegetable mixture around beef. Pass remaining dressing mixture.

Makes 4 servings (serving size: 1½ cups).

Nutritional Information Per Serving

Calories:	220	Protein (g):	23
Calories from total fat: 104		Carbohydrate (g):	6
(Calories from fat in beef: 55)		Cholesterol (mg):	58
Fat (g):	12	Sodium (mg):	409

BEEF & POTATO SALAD DIJON

Beef and the assertive flavor of Dijon-style mustard are perfect partners. Use leftover cooked steak or roast beef, or purchase what you need from the deli.

Total preparation and cooking time: 30 minutes

- ¾ pound cooked lean beef, sliced ⅛ inch thick and cut into 1-inch wide strips
- ¾ pound all-purpose potatoes
- ½ cup coarsely chopped onion
- 2½ tablespoons chopped fresh parsley
  Mixed salad greens

Mustard Dressing
- ¼ cup coarse-grain **or** regular Dijon-style mustard
- 2 tablespoons vegetable oil
- 1½ tablespoons white wine vinegar
- ¼ teaspoon salt
- ¼ teaspoon pepper

1. Cut potatoes into 1-inch pieces; place in saucepan and cover with cold water. Bring to a boil; cover and simmer 10 to 12 minutes or until tender. Drain potatoes.

2. Meanwhile in large bowl, combine dressing ingredients. Add hot potatoes to dressing; toss gently to coat. Cool.

3. Add beef, onion and parsley to potato mixture, mixing lightly. Serve immediately or cover and refrigerate. To serve, arrange salad greens on serving platter; top with beef mixture.

Makes 4 servings (serving size: 1½ cups).

Nutritional Information Per Serving

Calories:	339	Protein (g):	29
Calories from total fat: 145		Carbohydrate (g):	20
(Calories from fat in beef: 76)		Cholesterol (mg):	73
Fat (g):	16	Sodium (mg):	391

CURRIED BEEF & FRUIT SALAD

The salad can be made the night before; reserve the fruit to stir in just prior to serving. A simple yogurt-chutney dressing complements the deli roast beef and fruits.

Preparation time: 25 minutes
Chilling time: 1 hour

¾ pound deli roast beef, sliced ¼ inch thick

1 large apple, cut into ½-inch pieces

2 small nectarines **or** peaches, cut into ½-inch pieces

¾ cup chopped celery

¼ cup sliced green onions
  Boston **or** leaf lettuce

2 tablespoons slivered almonds, toasted (optional)

Curry-Yogurt Dressing

1 carton (8 ounces) nonfat plain yogurt

1½ tablespoons chopped Major Grey chutney

1 teaspoon curry powder

1. Stack beef slices; cut lengthwise in half and then crosswise into 1½-inch wide strips. In large bowl, combine beef, apple, nectarines, celery and onions; mix lightly.

2. In small bowl, combine dressing ingredients, mixing until well blended. Add to beef mixture; toss to coat. Cover and refrigerate at least 1 hour.

3. To serve, arrange lettuce on serving platter; top with beef mixture. Sprinkle with almonds, if desired.

Cook's Tip: Three-quarters pound leftover cooked beef steak or roast, sliced ¼ inch thick and cut into 1½-inch wide strips, may be substituted for deli roast beef.

Makes 4 servings (serving size: 1¼ cups).

Nutritional Information Per Serving

Calories:	269	Protein (g):	28
Calories from total fat: 58		Carbohydrate (g):	25
(Calories from fat in beef: 53)		Cholesterol (mg):	70
Fat (g):	6	Sodium (mg):	163

4.
30-MINUTE MEALS

 ood-for-you, good-tasting meals in 30 minutes? That's what this chapter is all about. These are the kinds of recipes that our busy lifestyles demand—quick foods with fabulous flavor.

With a few simple "quick-cooking" recipes and techniques in your repertoire, you can put a meal on the table for family—or guests—in less time than it takes for pizza delivery.

Key to 30-minute meals is learning to streamline preparation by using high quality prepared and convenience foods in tandem with fresh. Using your freezer and pantry to their full advantage can help:

- Frozen vegetables, quick-cooking beef cuts, a variety of breads, and ready-to-serve desserts are good to have on hand in the freezer.

- Spices and seasonings, pasta and grains, salad dressing and canned diced, seasoned tomatoes in the pantry will give you a head start on quick meals.

43

44

FIESTA PICADILLO

Spicy, quick picadillo is perfect over corn muffins, cornbread or spooned into flour tortillas. For a change of pace, try this spicy beef mixture over baked acorn squash quarters.

Total preparation and cooking time: 30 minutes

- 1 pound lean ground beef
- ½ cup chopped onion
- 1 clove garlic, crushed
- 1 jar (12 ounces) mild salsa
- ⅓ cup raisins
- 1 teaspoon ground cumin
- ¼ teaspoon ground cinnamon
- 4 corn muffins, warmed, split
- 1 tablespoon slivered almonds, toasted (optional)

1. In large nonstick skillet, brown ground beef, onion and garlic over medium heat 8 to 10 minutes or until beef is no longer pink, breaking up into ¾-inch crumbles. Pour off drippings.

2. Stir in salsa, raisins, cumin and cinnamon. Bring to a boil; reduce heat to medium-low. Cover and simmer 15 minutes, stirring occasionally.

3. Spoon equal amount of beef mixture over corn muffins. Garnish with almonds, if desired.

Makes 4 servings (serving size: ¼ of beef mixture and 1 corn muffin).

Nutritional Information Per Serving

Calories:	365	Protein (g):	24
Calories from total fat: 112		Carbohydrate (g):	39
(Calories from fat in beef: 82)		Cholesterol (mg):	88
Fat (g):	12	Sodium (mg):	780

SATAY-STYLE BEEF & PASTA

It's the flavors of satay without the skewers. Stir-fry strips of teriyaki marinated steak, then toss with vermicelli and a spicy peanut butter sauce.

Total preparation and cooking time: 30 minutes

- 1–pound boneless beef top sirloin **or** top round steak, cut 1 inch thick **or** flank steak
- 2 tablespoons prepared teriyaki sauce
- 6 ounces uncooked vermicelli **or** thin spaghetti
  Vegetable cooking spray
- ½ cup seeded and chopped cucumber

Peanut Butter Sauce

- 3 tablespoons prepared teriyaki sauce
- 2 tablespoons creamy peanut butter
- 1 tablespoon water
- ⅛ to ¼ teaspoon ground ginger
- ⅛ to ¼ teaspoon crushed red pepper

1. Trim fat from beef steak. Cut steak lengthwise in half and then crosswise into ⅛-inch thick strips. Add 2 tablespoons teriyaki sauce to beef; toss to coat.

2. Cook vermicelli according to package directions. Meanwhile in medium bowl, combine sauce ingredients, mixing until well blended. Add hot vermicelli; toss to coat. Keep warm.

3. Spray large nonstick skillet with cooking spray. Heat over medium-high heat until hot. Add beef (half at a time) and stir-fry 1 to 2 minutes or until outside surface is no longer pink. (Do not overcook.) Add to vermicelli mixture; toss lightly. Sprinkle with cucumber; serve immediately.

Makes 5 servings (serving size: ⅕ of recipe).

Nutritional Information Per Serving

Calories:	308	Protein (g):	27
Calories from total fat: 78		Carbohydrate (g):	29
(Calories from fat in beef: 44)		Cholesterol (mg):	61
Fat (g):	9	Sodium (mg):	767

LEMON PEPPER BEEF STEAK & POTATO WEDGES

Lemon pepper adds zesty flavor to the steak and potato wedges. Broil them together while you toss a salad and set the table. (See photograph)

Total preparation and cooking time: 30 minutes

1½–pound boneless beef top sirloin steak, cut
  1¼ inches thick

Steak Seasoning
  3 large cloves garlic, crushed
  2 teaspoons dried oregano leaves
  ½ teaspoon lemon pepper

Potato Wedges
  1 tablespoon olive oil
  ½ teaspoon lemon pepper
  3 all-purpose potatoes, each cut into 6
    lengthwise wedges

1. Combine steak seasoning ingredients; press into both sides of beef steak.

2. In medium bowl, combine oil and ½ teaspoon lemon pepper. Add potatoes; toss to coat.

3. Place steak on one side of rack in broiler pan so surface of meat is 3 to 4 inches from heat; arrange potatoes on the other side. Broil 18 to 20 minutes until steak is rare to medium doneness and potatoes are tender, turning steak and potato wedges once.

4. Trim fat from steak. Carve steak crosswise into slices and serve with potatoes.

Makes 6 servings (serving size: ⅙ of recipe).

Nutritional Information Per Serving

Calories:	233	Protein (g):	27
Calories from total fat: 77		Carbohydrate (g):	11
(Calories from fat in beef: 55)		Cholesterol (mg):	76
Fat (g):	9	Sodium (mg):	117

QUICK BEEF MINESTRONE SOUP

This convenient minestrone begins with Italian-flavored, recipe-ready tomatoes, frozen mixed vegetables and macaroni. Thin strips of beef steak are stirred into the hot soup during the 5-minute standing time—that's the only cooking they need! Crisp breadsticks make a great go-with.

Total preparation and cooking time: 30 minutes

- 1 pound beef round tip steaks, cut ⅛ to ¼ inch thick
- 3 cups water
- 1 package (10 ounces) frozen mixed vegetables
- 1 can (14½ ounces) Italian-style diced tomatoes, undrained
- ½ cup uncooked ditalini pasta **or** elbow macaroni
- 2 teaspoons instant beef bouillon granules
- ½ teaspoon dried basil leaves
  Grated Parmesan cheese (optional)

1. In 3-quart saucepan, combine water, vegetables, tomatoes, pasta, bouillon and basil. Bring to a boil; reduce heat to low. Simmer, uncovered, 10 minutes or until pasta is tender.

2. Meanwhile stack beef steaks; cut lengthwise in half and then crosswise into 1-inch wide strips.

3. Stir beef into simmering soup. Immediately remove from heat. Cover and let stand 5 minutes. Serve immediately; sprinkle with cheese, if desired.

Makes 4 servings (serving size: 1¾ cups).

Nutritional Information Per Serving

Calories:	290	Protein (g):	30
Calories from total fat: 59		Carbohydrate (g):	28
(Calories from fat in beef: 53)		Cholesterol (mg):	69
Fat (g):	7	Sodium (mg):	600

BEEF & VEGETABLE FRIED RICE

The next time you cook rice, make a double batch and freeze half of it for fried rice. Fresh ginger, garlic, sesame oil and soy sauce flavor this easy version made with ground beef, pea pods and red bell pepper. (See photograph)

Total preparation and cooking time: 25 minutes

1 pound lean ground beef
2 cloves garlic, crushed
1 teaspoon grated fresh ginger **or** ¼ teaspoon ground ginger
2 tablespoons water
1 large red bell pepper, cut into ½-inch pieces
1 package (6 ounces) frozen pea pods
3 cups cold cooked rice
3 tablespoons reduced-sodium soy sauce
2 teaspoons dark sesame oil
¼ cup thinly sliced green onions

1. In large nonstick skillet, brown ground beef, garlic and ginger over medium heat 8 to 10 minutes or until beef is no longer pink, breaking up into ¾-inch crumbles. Remove with slotted spoon; pour off drippings.

2. In same skillet, heat water over medium-high heat until hot. Add bell pepper and pea pods; cook 3 minutes or until water is evaporated and bell pepper is crisp-tender, stirring occasionally. Add rice, soy sauce and sesame oil; mix well. Return beef to skillet; heat through, about 5 minutes. Stir in green onions before serving.

Makes 4 servings (serving size: 1½ cups).

Nutritional Information Per Serving

Calories:	428	Protein (g):	29
Calories from total fat: 108		Carbohydrate (g):	50
(Calories from fat in beef: 82)		Cholesterol (mg):	70
Fat (g):	12	Sodium (mg):	517

BBQ Beef & Potato Hash

It's "hash in a flash" when you begin with deli roast beef (or leftover roast beef) and frozen potatoes O'Brien. Colorful bell pepper and bits of onion team up with prepared barbecue sauce to add just the right "zip."

Total preparation and cooking time: 30 minutes

¾ pound cooked beef, cut into ½-inch pieces
2 tablespoons vegetable oil
3 cups frozen potatoes O'Brien
1 cup chopped green, red **or** yellow bell pepper
½ cup chopped onion
¼ teaspoon pepper
¼ cup prepared barbecue sauce **or** beef gravy

1. In large nonstick skillet, heat oil over medium-high heat until hot. Add potatoes, bell pepper and onion; cook 10 to 15 minutes or until potatoes are browned and crisp, stirring occasionally.

2. Add beef and pepper; mix lightly. Stir in barbecue sauce and continue cooking 2 to 3 minutes or until heated through.

Makes 4 servings (serving size: 1 cup).

Nutritional Information Per Serving

Calories:	363	Protein (g):	28
Calories from total fat: 119		Carbohydrate (g):	33
(Calories from fat in beef: 53)		Cholesterol (mg):	69
Fat (g):	13	Sodium (mg):	236

EASY BEEF SAUSAGE & BLACK BEAN SOUP

Hearty black bean soup is a cold weather favorite. This version is 30-minutes-quick when you start with canned black bean soup. Jazz it up with carrots, celery and smoked beef sausage. No one will ever guess!

Total preparation and cooking time: 30 minutes

- ½ pound reduced-fat fully-cooked smoked beef sausage link
- 1 cup thinly sliced carrots
- 1 cup thinly sliced celery
- ¾ cup water
- 2 cans (19 ounces each) black bean soup
  Nonfat plain yogurt
  Chopped fresh parsley

1. In 3-quart saucepan, combine carrots, celery and water. Bring to a boil; reduce heat to low. Cover and simmer 5 minutes or until vegetables are crisp-tender.

2. Meanwhile cut beef sausage lengthwise in half and then crosswise into ½-inch thick slices. Add sausage and soup to vegetables, stirring to blend. Bring to a boil; reduce heat to low. Simmer, uncovered, 10 minutes, stirring occasionally.

3. Serve with yogurt and parsley.

Cook's Tip: Two cans (19 ounces each) lentil soup may be substituted for black bean soup.

Makes 6 servings (serving size: 1 cup).

Nutritional Information Per Serving

Calories:	195	Protein (g):	12
Calories from total fat: 77		Carbohydrate (g):	26
(Calories from fat in beef: 66)		Cholesterol (mg):	26
Fat (g):	9	Sodium (mg):	917

ZUCCHINI BEEF & PASTA SUPPER

How easy does it get? The pasta doesn't need to be precooked for this Italian-inspired beef, zucchini and tomato skillet dinner. Serve with breadsticks or garlic bread.

Total preparation and cooking time: 30 minutes

- 1 pound lean ground beef
- 1 medium onion, chopped
- 1 clove garlic, crushed
- ½ teaspoon salt
- 1 can (13¾ to 14½ ounces) ready-to-serve beef broth
- 1 teaspoon Italian seasoning
- ⅛ teaspoon ground red pepper
- 2 cups sliced zucchini, cut ½ inch thick
- 1 cup uncooked farfalle (bow tie) pasta
- 2 plum tomatoes, each cut into 4 wedges
- 2 tablespoons grated Parmesan cheese

1. In large nonstick skillet, brown ground beef, onion and garlic over medium heat 8 to 10 minutes or until beef is no longer pink, breaking up into 1-inch crumbles. Remove beef with slotted spoon; pour off drippings. Season beef with salt; set aside.

2. In same skillet, add broth, Italian seasoning, red pepper, zucchini and pasta, pushing pasta into liquid. Bring to a boil; reduce heat to medium. Simmer, uncovered, 15 minutes or until pasta is tender, stirring occasionally.

3. Return beef to skillet and add tomatoes; heat through. Sprinkle with cheese.

Makes 4 servings (serving size: 1½ cups).

Nutritional Information Per Serving

Calories:	296	Protein (g):	28
Calories from total fat: 98		Carbohydrate (g):	22
(Calories from fat in beef: 82)		Cholesterol (mg):	72
Fat (g):	11	Sodium (mg):	715

STEAK WITH SPICY POTATOES

While the seasoned steak and potatoes broil, prepare a vegetable side dish in the microwave or on the stove top. Use convenient frozen vegetables or purchase favorites such as broccoli from the produce section that are pre-washed, trimmed and ready-to-cook.

Total preparation and cooking time: 30 minutes

1–pound boneless beef top sirloin steak, cut
   1 inch thick
   Vegetable cooking spray
2 large all-purpose potatoes, cut diagonally into
   ½-inch thick slices
1 tablespoon olive oil
1 teaspoon Spicy Seasoning Mix (see page 39)
   Salt (optional)

1. Spray rack of broiler pan with cooking spray. Place steak on one side of rack in broiler pan so surface of meat is 3 to 4 inches from heat; arrange potatoes on the other side. Combine oil and seasoning mix; brush potatoes with half of the mixture.

2. Broil 16 to 18 minutes until steak is rare to medium doneness and potatoes are tender, turning steak and potatoes once; brush potatoes with remaining seasoned oil.

3. Trim fat from steak. Carve steak crosswise into slices. Season steak and potatoes with salt, if desired.

Makes 4 servings (serving size: ¼ of recipe).

Nutritional Information Per Serving

Calories:	283	Protein (g):	28
Calories from total fat: 87		Carbohydrate (g):	20
(Calories from fat in beef: 55)		Cholesterol (mg):	76
Fat (g):	10	Sodium (mg):	67

ITALIAN BEEF STIR-FRY WITH PASTA

Fat-free Italian salad dressing does double duty—it adds zesty flavor to the stir-fry and doubles as a ready-made sauce.

Total preparation and cooking time: 30 minutes

- 1 pound beef round tip steaks, cut ⅛ to ¼ inch thick
- 1½ cups uncooked medium shell **or** farfalle (bow tie) pasta
- 1 tablespoon olive oil
- 2 cloves garlic, crushed
- ¼ teaspoon salt
- ⅛ teaspoon pepper
- 3 cups (8 ounces) sliced mushrooms
- 1 cup cherry tomato halves
- ¼ cup prepared fat-free Italian dressing
- 1 tablespoon grated Parmesan cheese
- 1 tablespoon chopped fresh Italian parsley

1. Cook pasta according to package directions. Keep warm.

2. Meanwhile stack beef steaks; cut lengthwise in half and then crosswise into 1-inch wide strips. In large nonstick skillet, heat oil over medium-high heat until hot. Add beef and garlic (half at a time) and stir-fry 1 minute or until outside surface is no longer pink. (Do not overcook.) Season with salt and pepper. Remove from skillet with slotted spoon; keep warm.

3. In same skillet, add mushrooms; stir-fry 3 minutes or until tender. Return beef to skillet and add tomatoes and dressing; heat through.

4. Spoon beef mixture over hot pasta; sprinkle with cheese and parsley.

Makes 4 servings (serving size: 1½ cups).

Nutritional Information Per Serving

Calories:	356	Protein (g):	31
Calories from total fat: 96		Carbohydrate (g):	33
(Calories from fat in beef: 53)		Cholesterol (mg):	71
Fat (g):	11	Sodium (mg):	448

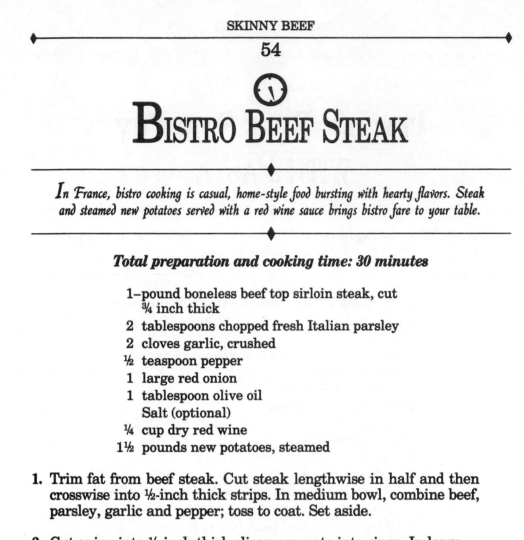

BISTRO BEEF STEAK

In France, bistro cooking is casual, home-style food bursting with hearty flavors. Steak and steamed new potatoes served with a red wine sauce brings bistro fare to your table.

Total preparation and cooking time: 30 minutes

1–pound boneless beef top sirloin steak, cut
  ¾ inch thick
2 tablespoons chopped fresh Italian parsley
2 cloves garlic, crushed
½ teaspoon pepper
1 large red onion
1 tablespoon olive oil
  Salt (optional)
¼ cup dry red wine
1½ pounds new potatoes, steamed

1. Trim fat from beef steak. Cut steak lengthwise in half and then crosswise into ½-inch thick strips. In medium bowl, combine beef, parsley, garlic and pepper; toss to coat. Set aside.

2. Cut onion into ¼-inch thick slices; separate into rings. In large nonstick skillet, heat oil over medium-high heat until hot. Add onion; cook and stir 3 to 5 minutes or until crisp-tender. Remove to serving platter; keep warm.

3. In same skillet, add beef and stir-fry 2 minutes or until outside surface is no longer pink. Season with salt, if desired. Place beef on top of onion.

4. Add wine to skillet; cook and stir until browned bits attached to skillet are dissolved and liquid thickens slightly. Pour sauce over beef and onions. Serve with potatoes.

Cook's Tip: To steam new potatoes, place steamer basket in ½ inch water (water should not touch bottom of basket). Place 10 to 12 new potatoes (about 1½ pounds) in basket. Cover tightly and heat to boiling; reduce heat. Steam 18 to 22 minutes or until tender.

Makes 4 servings (serving size: ¼ of recipe).

Nutritional Information Per Serving

Calories:	406	Protein (g):	31
Calories from total fat: 87		Carbohydrate (g):	46
(Calories from fat in beef: 55)		Cholesterol (mg):	76
Fat (g):	10	Sodium (mg):	73

Step 1. **Trim fat from steak.**

Step 2. **Cut steak lengthwise in half.**

Step 3. **Cut crosswise into thin strips.**

STIR-FRIED SIRLOIN & SPINACH WITH NOODLES

Stir-fried strips of steak marinated in Oriental flavors join spinach and vermicelli for a dish that's guaranteed to rival your favorite Chinese carry-out. Look for pre-washed spinach in the produce section or supermarket salad bar to save time. (See photograph)

Total preparation and cooking time: 30 minutes

- 1–pound boneless beef top sirloin steak, cut 1 inch thick
- 4 ounces uncooked vermicelli **or** thin spaghetti
- 1 package (10 ounces) fresh spinach leaves, rinsed and stems removed, thinly sliced
- 1 cup fresh bean sprouts
- ¼ cup sliced green onions

Marinade
- ¼ cup hoisin sauce
- 2 tablespoons reduced-sodium soy sauce
- 1 tablespoon water
- 2 teaspoons dark sesame oil
- 2 cloves garlic, crushed
- ⅛ to ¼ teaspoon crushed red pepper

1. Trim fat from beef steak. Cut steak lengthwise in half and then crosswise into ⅛-inch thick strips. Combine marinade ingredients; pour half over beef. Cover and marinate in refrigerator 10 minutes. Reserve remaining marinade.

2. Meanwhile cook vermicelli according to package directions.

3. Remove beef from marinade; discard marinade. Heat large nonstick skillet over medium-high heat until hot. Add beef (half at a time) and stir-fry 1 to 2 minutes or until outside surface is no longer pink. (Do not overcook.) Remove from skillet with slotted spoon; keep warm.

4. In same skillet, combine vermicelli, spinach, bean sprouts, green onions and reserved marinade; cook until spinach is wilted and mixture is heated through, stirring occasionally. Return beef to skillet; mix lightly.

Makes 4 servings (serving size: 1½ cups).

Nutritional Information Per Serving

Calories:	331	Protein (g):	33
Calories from total fat: 85		Carbohydrate (g):	28
(Calories from fat in beef: 55)		Cholesterol (mg):	76
Fat (g):	10	Sodium (mg):	540

SPANISH STEAK WITH SAUTÉED VEGETABLES

Family or guests will appreciate this easy, flavorful dinner. One skillet is all it takes to cook the seasoned steaks and stir-fry the bell pepper and onion accompaniment.

Total preparation and cooking time: 30 minutes

1–pound boneless beef top sirloin steak, cut
¾ inch thick
½ teaspoon garlic powder
¼ teaspoon pepper
Vegetable cooking spray
⅛ teaspoon salt
2 tablespoons drained, canned chopped green chilies
1 tablespoon dairy sour half-and-half

Sautéed Vegetables
1 teaspoon vegetable oil
2 green **or** red bell peppers, cut lengthwise into thin strips
1 small onion, thinly sliced
2 tablespoons coarsely chopped walnuts
½ teaspoon garlic powder
¼ teaspoon salt
¼ teaspoon chili powder

1. Trim fat from beef steak. Cut steak crosswise into 4 pieces. Combine ½ teaspoon garlic powder and pepper; sprinkle evenly over steak pieces. Spray large nonstick skillet with cooking spray. Heat skillet over medium-high heat until hot. Place beef in skillet and cook 8 to 10 minutes for rare to medium doneness, turning once. Remove to warm platter; season with ⅛ teaspoon salt.

2. In same skillet, heat oil until hot. Add bell peppers, onion and walnuts; cook and stir 2 minutes. Combine ½ teaspoon garlic powder, ¼ teaspoon salt and chili powder; sprinkle over vegetables and continue cooking 2 minutes, stirring frequently.

3. In small bowl, combine chilies and sour half-and-half. To serve, place a dollop of chili mixture on each piece of steak. Spoon vegetables around steaks.

Makes 4 servings (serving size: 1 piece steak and ¾ cup vegetables).

Nutritional Information Per Serving

Calories:	225	Protein (g):	27
Calories from total fat: 91		Carbohydrate (g):	6
(Calories from fat in beef: 55)		Cholesterol (mg):	77
Fat (g):	10	Sodium (mg):	262

Step 1. **Trim fat from steak.**

Step 2. **Cut steak crosswise into four pieces.**

THAI BEEF & NOODLE TOSS

Ramen noodles are instant-style Oriental noodles that cook in just minutes— a perfect companion for quick-cooking round tip steaks. Add the amount of jalapeños you like for heat.

Total preparation and cooking time: 25 minutes

- 1 pound beef round tip steaks, cut ⅛ to ¼ inch thick
- 1 to 2 jalapeño peppers, finely chopped
- 1 tablespoon vegetable oil
- 1 package (3 ounces) beef-flavored instant ramen noodles
- ¼ cup prepared steak sauce
- 1 medium carrot, shredded
- 2 tablespoons chopped fresh cilantro **or** parsley
- ¼ cup unsalted roasted peanuts (optional)

1. Stack beef steaks; cut lengthwise in half and then crosswise into 1-inch wide strips. In medium bowl, combine beef, jalapeño peppers and oil; toss to coat.

2. Break noodles into 3 or 4 pieces; reserve seasoning packet. Cook noodles according to package directions; drain.

3. Meanwhile heat large nonstick skillet over medium-high heat until hot. Add beef (half at a time) and stir-fry 1 minute or until outside surface is no longer pink. (Do not overcook.) Remove from skillet; keep warm.

4. In same skillet, combine noodles, steak sauce, carrot, cilantro and reserved seasoning packet. Cook over medium heat until heated through, stirring occasionally. Return beef to skillet; mix lightly. Garnish with peanuts, if desired. Serve immediately.

Cook's Tip: Remove interior ribs and seeds from jalapeño peppers if a milder flavor is desired.

Makes 4 servings (serving size: ¼ of recipe).

Nutritional Information Per Serving

Calories:	315	Protein (g):	28
Calories from total fat: 122		Carbohydrate (g):	20
(Calories from fat in beef: 53)		Cholesterol (mg):	69
Fat (g):	14	Sodium (mg):	806

MUFFIN TIN MEATLOAVES & QUICK PARMESAN MASHED POTATOES

A guaranteed family pleaser. Mini-meatloaves baked in a muffin pan are studded with shredded zucchini. A brushing of ketchup forms a glaze as they bake. Or, for a change of pace, brush with prepared barbecue sauce. Serve with carrots and Parmesan Mashed Potatoes.

Total preparation and cooking time: 30 minutes

- 1½ pounds lean ground beef
- 1½ cups shredded zucchini
- 1 cup soft bread crumbs
- 1 egg, slightly beaten
- 1 teaspoon Italian seasoning
- ½ teaspoon salt
- ¼ cup ketchup

1. Heat oven to 400°. In a large bowl, combine all ingredients except ketchup, mixing lightly but thoroughly. Place approximately ⅓ cup beef mixture into each of 12 medium muffin cups, pressing lightly; spread ketchup over tops.

2. Bake in 400° oven 20 minutes or until no longer pink and juices run clear.

3. Meanwhile prepare Quick Parmesan Mashed Potatoes. Remove meatloaves from pan; serve with potatoes.

Quick Parmesan Mashed Potatoes

- 1½ pounds all-purpose potatoes, scrubbed, quartered
- 3 tablespoons water
- 3 large cloves garlic, crushed
- ⅓ cup low-fat milk
- 3 tablespoons grated Parmesan cheese
- ¾ teaspoon salt

1. In 2-quart microwave-safe container, combine potatoes, water and garlic. Cover and microwave at high 12 to 14 minutes or until potatoes are tender.

2. Mash potatoes until smooth. Add milk, cheese and salt, beating until light and fluffy. (If mixture becomes too thick, add additional milk, 1 tablespoon at a time.)

Cook's Tip: To make soft bread crumbs, place torn bread slices in food processor fitted with steel blade, or blender container. Cover; process 30 seconds, pulsing on and off until fine crumbs. One and a half slices will yield 1 cup soft bread crumbs.

Makes 6 servings (serving size: 2 mini-meatloaves and ½ cup potatoes).

Nutritional Information Per Serving

Calories:	330	Protein (g):	28
Calories from total fat: 105		Carbohydrate (g):	29
(Calories from fat in beef: 82)		Cholesterol (mg):	109
Fat (g):	12	Sodium (mg):	768

CURRIED BEEF & VEGETABLE PILAF

Curry powder flavors this 30-minute meal-in-one combo. An accompaniment of seasonal fresh fruit will complete the meal.

Total preparation and cooking time: 30 minutes

1	pound lean ground beef
1½	cups water
⅔	cup uncooked regular long grain rice
1	teaspoon curry powder
½	teaspoon salt
1	package (10 ounces) frozen peas and carrots, defrosted
⅓	cup raisins
1	large onion, chopped
2	cloves garlic, crushed
1	teaspoon curry powder
½	teaspoon salt
⅛	teaspoon ground red pepper
¼	cup slivered almonds, toasted (optional)

1. In 2-quart saucepan, bring water to a boil. Stir in rice, 1 teaspoon curry powder and ½ teaspoon salt. Reduce heat to medium-low. Cover tightly and simmer 15 minutes.

2. Stir in peas and carrots and raisins; continue cooking, covered, 10 minutes or until rice is tender.

3. Meanwhile in large nonstick skillet, brown ground beef, onion and garlic over medium heat 8 to 10 minutes or until beef is no longer pink, breaking up into ¾-inch crumbles. Pour off drippings. Stir in 1 teaspoon curry powder, ½ teaspoon salt and red pepper; cook 2 minutes.

4. Add rice mixture to skillet; mix well and heat through. Garnish with almonds, if desired.

Makes 4 servings (serving size: 1¾ cups).

Nutritional Information Per Serving

Calories:	400	Protein (g):	28
Calories from total fat: 90		Carbohydrate (g):	51
(Calories from fat in beef: 82)		Cholesterol (mg):	70
Fat (g):	10	Sodium (mg):	662

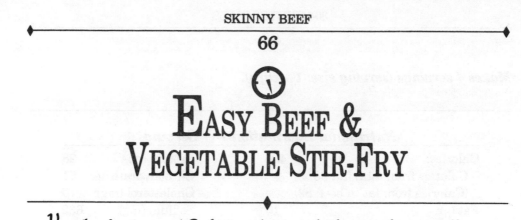

EASY BEEF & VEGETABLE STIR-FRY

Versatile and a time-saver! Beef strips cook in a couple of minutes; frozen vegetables are ready to use—no chopping required! Vary the stir-fry with different vegetable combos.

Total preparation and cooking time: 30 minutes

1–pound beef top round **or** boneless top sirloin steak, cut 1 inch thick **or** flank steak
1 tablespoon vegetable oil
1 clove garlic, crushed
2 tablespoons water
1 package (16 ounces) frozen vegetable mixture
2 cups hot cooked rice
⅓ cup coarsely chopped walnuts, toasted (optional)

Sauce
¼ cup water
2 tablespoons dry sherry
2 tablespoons reduced-sodium soy sauce
1 tablespoon cornstarch

1. Trim fat from beef steak. Cut steak lengthwise in half and then crosswise into ⅛-inch thick strips; reserve.

2. In small bowl, combine sauce ingredients; reserve.

3. In large nonstick skillet, heat oil over medium-high heat until hot. Add beef and garlic (half at a time) and stir-fry 1 to 2 minutes or until outside surface is no longer pink. (Do not overcook.) Remove from skillet with slotted spoon; keep warm.

4. In same skillet, heat 2 tablespoons water until hot. Add vegetables; cook 5 minutes or until water is evaporated and vegetables are hot, stirring occasionally. Return beef to skillet and add sauce mixture; cook and stir until sauce is thickened and bubbly. Serve over rice; sprinkle with walnuts, if desired.

Makes 4 servings (serving size: ¼ of recipe).

Nutritional Information Per Serving

Calories:	415	Protein (g):	33
Calories from total fat: 104		Carbohydrate (g):	40
(Calories from fat in beef: 38)		Cholesterol (mg):	84
Fat (g):	12	Sodium (mg):	679

Step 1. **Trim fat from steak.**

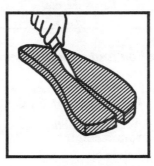

Step 2. **Cut steak lengthwise in half.**

Step 3. **Cut crosswise into thin strips.**

■ **Stir-fry meat (half at a time) in a skillet or wok over medium-high heat.**

■ **Continuously turn meat pieces with a scooping motion.**

MEXICAN BEEF STIR-FRY OVER SPICY RICE

Stir-fry goes Mexican. A blend of cumin, garlic and oregano seasons the steak which is teamed with mild red bell pepper and spicy hot jalapeno. Homemade Spicy Seasoning Mix flavors the rice.

Total preparation and cooking time: 30 minutes

- 1–pound beef top round **or** boneless top sirloin steak, cut 1 inch thick **or** flank steak
- 2 tablespoons vegetable oil
- 1 teaspoon ground cumin
- 1 teaspoon garlic salt
- 1 teaspoon dried oregano leaves
- 1 red bell pepper, cut into thin strips
- 1 medium onion, chopped
- 1 to 2 jalapeño peppers, seeded, cut into thin strips
- 1 tablespoon chopped fresh cilantro **or** parsley

Spicy Rice
- 1 cup uncooked regular long grain rice
- 1 teaspoon Spicy Seasoning Mix (see page 39)

1. Cook rice according to package directions, adding seasoning mix to water.

2. Meanwhile trim fat from beef steak. Cut steak lengthwise in half and then crosswise into ⅛-inch thick strips.

3. In small bowl, combine oil, cumin, garlic salt and oregano. In large nonstick skillet, heat 1 tablespoon seasoned oil over medium-high heat until hot. Add bell pepper, onion and jalapeño peppers; stir-fry 3 minutes or until crisp-tender. Remove from skillet; reserve.

4. In same skillet, heat remaining seasoned oil until hot. Add beef (half at a time) and stir-fry 1 to 2 minutes or until outside surface is no longer pink. (Do not overcook.) Return vegetables to skillet; heat through. Serve over rice. Garnish with cilantro.

Makes 4 servings (serving size: 1 cup beef mixture and ½ cup rice).

Nutritional Information Per Serving

Calories:	407	Protein (g):	31
Calories from total fat: 104		Carbohydrate (g):	43
(Calories from fat in beef: 38)		Cholesterol (mg):	71
Fat (g):	12	Sodium (mg):	523

Canton Beef with Pineapple

Beef, pineapple and bell pepper in a classic Oriental-style sauce is ready quicker than carry-out. Stir-fry the peppers in water instead of oil—they're fresher tasting and maintain their bright color better.

Total preparation and cooking time: 30 minutes

- 1 pound boneless beef top sirloin **or** tenderloin steaks, cut ¾ inch thick
- 1 tablespoon reduced-sodium soy sauce
- ½ teaspoon cornstarch
  Dash pepper
- 2 tablespoons water
- 2 red **or** green bell peppers, cut into ¾-inch pieces
- 1 clove garlic, crushed
- 1 tablespoon vegetable oil
- 1 can (8 ounces) pineapple chunks in juice, drained
- 2 cups hot cooked rice

Sauce
- 3 tablespoons ketchup
- 2 tablespoons sugar
- 1 tablespoon reduced-sodium soy sauce
- 1 teaspoon Worcestershire sauce

1. Trim fat from beef steak; cut steak into ¾-inch cubes. In medium bowl, combine 1 tablespoon soy sauce, cornstarch and pepper; add beef and toss to coat.

2. In small bowl, combine sauce ingredients; set aside.

3. In large skillet, heat water over medium-high heat until hot. Add bell peppers and garlic; cook and stir 3 to 4 minutes or until water is evaporated and bell peppers are crisp-tender. Remove from skillet; set aside.

4. In same skillet, heat oil until hot. Add beef (half at a time) and stir-fry 3 minutes or until outside surface is no longer pink. Stir in sauce mixture, bell peppers and pineapple; heat through. Serve over rice.

Makes 4 servings (serving size: 1 cup beef mixture and ½ cup rice).

Nutritional Information Per Serving

Calories:	405	Protein (g):	30
Calories from total fat: 90		Carbohydrate (g):	47
(Calories from fat in beef: 55)		Cholesterol (mg):	76
Fat (g):	10	Sodium (mg):	521

SALSA CHILI & CHEESE POTATO TOPPER

While the potatoes "micro-bake," simmer up a quick chili topper made with ground beef, picante sauce and bell pepper. Remember that the heat in picante sauce will intensify when cooked.

Total preparation and cooking time: 25 minutes

- 1 pound lean ground beef
- 2 large baking potatoes
- 1 medium green bell pepper, cut into ½-inch pieces
- ½ cup chopped onion
- 1 cup prepared medium picante sauce **or** salsa
  Salt (optional)
- ½ cup shredded Cheddar cheese (optional)
- 2 green onions, sliced

1. Pierce potatoes with fork. Microwave at high 8 to 10 minutes or until tender, rotating ¼ turn after 4 minutes. Let stand 5 minutes.

2. Meanwhile in large nonstick skillet, brown ground beef, bell pepper and onion over medium heat 8 to 10 minutes or until beef is no longer pink, breaking up into ¾-inch crumbles. Pour off drippings. Stir in picante sauce; heat through, stirring occasionally.

3. Cut potatoes lengthwise in half; break up and fluff pulp with fork. Season with salt, if desired. Spoon equal amount of beef mixture over each potato half. Top each with equal amounts of cheese, if desired, and green onions.

Makes 4 servings (serving size: ½ potato with ¾ cup topping).

Nutritional Information Per Serving

Calories:	295	Protein (g):	25
Calories from total fat: 84		Carbohydrate (g):	28
(Calories from fat in beef: 82)		Cholesterol (mg):	70
Fat (g):	9	Sodium (mg):	535

5.
BURGERS AND OTHER HAND-HELD FAVORITES

Everyone loves a sandwich. But sandwiches just aren't what they used to be. They're more! Today's "hand-held" favorites span the gamut from burgers to burritos.

The recipes in this chapter are perfect for families on the go. Updated sloppy joes, barbecue and Italian beef share the spotlight with quesadillas and moo shu beef. "Holders" include traditional breads and rolls as well as more innovative choices such as tortillas, pita bread, even lettuce leaves!

Easy accompaniments are in order for these 90s'-style sandwiches. Pick up salads and coleslaw from the deli and fresh fruits from the supermarket salad bar.

15-Minute Beef Barbecue

Barbecue almost instantly! Thin steak strips cook completely in just a minute; add prepared barbecue sauce and heat through. Coleslaw from the deli rounds out the meal.

Total preparation and cooking time: 15 minutes

- 1 pound beef round tip steaks, cut ⅛ to ¼ inch thick
- 2 teaspoons vegetable oil
- 1 medium onion, cut into thin wedges
- ¾ cup prepared barbecue sauce
- 4 crusty rolls, split

1. Stack beef steaks; cut lengthwise in half and then crosswise into 1-inch wide strips. Set aside.

2. In large nonstick skillet, heat oil over medium-high heat until hot. Add onion; cook and stir 3 minutes or until lightly browned. Remove from skillet; keep warm.

3. In same skillet, add beef (half at a time) and stir-fry 1 minute or until outside surface is no longer pink. (Do not overcook.) Stir in onion and barbecue sauce; heat through, stirring occasionally.

4. Spoon equal amount of beef mixture on bottom half of each roll; close with top half of roll.

Makes 4 servings (serving size: 1 sandwich).

Nutritional Information Per Serving

Calories:	348	Protein (g):	29
Calories from total fat: 93		Carbohydrate (g):	32
(Calories from fat in beef: 53)		Cholesterol (mg):	70
Fat (g):	10	Sodium (mg):	688

ZESTY BASIL BURGERS

Basil Mayonnaise (a blend of mayo, basil and Dijon-style mustard) is delicious teamed with juicy hamburgers on crusty rolls.

Total preparation and cooking time: 30 minutes

- 1 pound lean ground beef
- 3 tablespoons finely chopped onion
- 1 clove garlic, crushed
- ¾ teaspoon salt
- ¼ teaspoon pepper
- 4 crusty rolls, split
- 1 cup packed spinach leaves
- 4 tomato slices

Basil Mayonnaise
- 3 tablespoons reduced-calorie mayonnaise
- 1 tablespoon chopped fresh basil **or** 1 teaspoon dried basil leaves
- 1 teaspoon Dijon-style mustard

1. In medium bowl, combine ground beef, onion, garlic, salt and pepper, mixing lightly but thoroughly. Shape into four oval ½-inch thick patties.

2. Heat large nonstick skillet over medium heat until hot. Place patties in skillet; cook 7 to 8 minutes or until no longer pink and juices run clear, turning once.

3. Meanwhile in small bowl, combine Basil Mayonnaise ingredients; mix well.

4. Line bottom half of each roll with spinach and tomato. Place burger on tomato; top with 1 tablespoon mayonnaise mixture. Close with top half of roll.

Makes 4 servings (serving size: 1 sandwich).

Nutritional Information Per Serving

Calories:	332	Protein (g):	26
Calories from total fat: 134		Carbohydrate (g):	24
(Calories from fat in beef: 82)		Cholesterol (mg):	76
Fat (g):	15	Sodium (mg):	762

Moo Shu Beef

Moo shu beef made easy! Use flour tortillas for the "wrapper" and packaged coleslaw mix in the filling. (See photograph)

Total preparation and cooking time: 30 minutes

- 1–pound boneless beef top sirloin **or** top round steak, cut ¾ inch thick **or** flank steak
- 1 cup hot water
- ½ ounce dried shiitake mushrooms (optional)
- 3 cups packaged coleslaw mix
- ⅔ cup sliced green onions
- 1 tablespoon cornstarch, dissolved in ¼ cup water
- 8 flour tortillas (each about 8 inches), warmed
- ⅓ cup hoisin sauce

Marinade
- 2 tablespoons reduced-sodium soy sauce
- 2 tablespoons water
- 1 tablespoon dark sesame oil
- 2 cloves garlic, crushed
- 2 teaspoons sugar

1. Trim fat from beef steak. Cut steak lengthwise in half and then crosswise into thin strips. Stack 3 to 4 strips; cut lengthwise in half to form thinner strips.

2. In medium bowl, combine marinade ingredients; add beef, tossing to coat. Cover and marinate in refrigerator 20 minutes.

3. Meanwhile in small bowl, pour hot water over mushrooms; let stand 20 minutes or until mushrooms are softened. Drain well. Remove stems; cut mushrooms into thin strips.

4. Remove beef from marinade; discard marinade. Heat large nonstick skillet over medium-high heat until hot. Add beef (half at a time) and stir-fry 1 to 2 minutes or until outside surface is no longer pink. (Do not overcook.) Add mushrooms, coleslaw mix, green onions and cornstarch mixture. Cook and stir until sauce is thickened and bubbly.

5. To assemble, spread one side of each tortilla with 2 teaspoons hoisin sauce. Spoon about ½ cup beef mixture in center of each tortilla. Fold bottom edge up over filling. Fold right and left sides to center, overlapping edges.

Cook's Tip: Thinly sliced green cabbage may be substituted for packaged coleslaw mix.

Makes 4 servings (serving size: 2 filled tortillas).

Nutritional Information Per Serving

Calories:	484	Protein (g):	34
Calories from total fat: 126		Carbohydrate (g):	56
(Calories from fat in beef: 55)		Cholesterol (mg):	76
Fat (g):	14	Sodium (mg):	722

Shortcut Italian Beef Sandwiches

No need to spend hours preparing a roast for Italian beef sandwiches! While the seasoned broth simmers, sauté onion and bell peppers, then the round tip steaks. Dip cut sides of Italian rolls into the savory broth, then pile high with beef and veggies.

Total preparation and cooking time: 20 minutes

- 1 pound beef round tip steaks, cut ¼ inch thick
- 1 cup ready-to-serve beef broth
- ¼ teaspoon dried oregano leaves
- 1 tablespoon vegetable oil
- 2 small green bell peppers, cut into thin strips
- 1 medium onion, sliced
- 2 cloves garlic, crushed
- ¼ teaspoon dried oregano leaves
- 4 Italian rolls, split

1. In small saucepan, combine broth and ¼ teaspoon oregano; simmer 10 to 15 minutes.

2. Meanwhile in large nonstick skillet, heat oil over medium-high heat until hot. Add bell peppers, onion, garlic and ¼ teaspoon oregano; cook and stir 3 to 4 minutes or until tender. Remove from skillet; keep warm.

3. In same skillet, cook steaks (half at a time) 1 to 1½ minutes or until outside surface is no longer pink, turning once.

4. Dip cut surface of bottom half of each roll in broth; top with steak and equal amounts of vegetables. Dip cut surface of top half of each roll in broth; close sandwiches.

Makes 4 servings (serving size: 1 sandwich).

Nutritional Information Per Serving

Calories:	377	Protein (g):	33
Calories from total fat: 99		Carbohydrate (g):	35
(Calories from fat in beef: 53)		Cholesterol (mg):	70
Fat (g):	11	Sodium (mg):	664

CONFETTI SLOPPY JOES

Barbecue sauce, onion and ground beef form the basis for 20-minute sloppy joes. Corn and green bell peppers add color and crunch. Accompany with a fresh fruit salad.

Total preparation and cooking time: 20 minutes

- 1 pound lean ground beef
- 1 small onion, chopped
- ¾ cup prepared barbecue sauce
- ½ cup frozen corn, defrosted
- ¼ teaspoon salt
- ⅛ teaspoon pepper
- 4 hamburger buns, split
- ½ cup chopped green bell pepper

1. In large nonstick skillet, brown ground beef and onion over medium heat 8 to 10 minutes or until beef is no longer pink, breaking up into ¾-inch crumbles. Pour off drippings. Stir in barbecue sauce, corn, salt and pepper; heat through, stirring occasionally.

2. Spoon equal amount of beef mixture on bottom half of each bun; top with bell pepper. Close with top half of bun.

Makes 4 servings (serving size: 1 sandwich).

Nutritional Information Per Serving

Calories:	350	Protein (g):	27
Calories from total fat: 112		Carbohydrate (g):	34
(Calories from fat in beef: 82)		Cholesterol (mg):	72
Fat (g):	12	Sodium (mg):	786

SPICY ORANGE BEEF LETTUCE PACKETS

A unique way to eat stir-fry—wrapped in a lettuce leaf! If you prefer, substitute a flour tortilla or pita bread for the lettuce. (See photograph)

Total preparation and cooking time: 20 minutes

- 1–pound beef top round **or** boneless top sirloin steak, cut ¾ inch thick **or** flank steak
- 2 teaspoons cornstarch
- 1 tablespoon vegetable oil
- ¼ teaspoon crushed red pepper
- 1 cup shredded carrot
- ½ cup thinly sliced green onions
- 2 heads Boston lettuce (about 16 leaves)

Sauce
- 2 tablespoons frozen orange juice concentrate, defrosted
- 2 tablespoons hoisin sauce
- 2 tablespoons rice wine vinegar
- 2 tablespoons soy sauce
- 2 teaspoons cornstarch

1. Trim fat from beef steak. Cut steak lengthwise in half and then crosswise into ⅛-inch thick strips. In medium bowl, combine beef and 2 teaspoons cornstarch; toss to coat. Set aside.

2. In small bowl, combine sauce ingredients; set aside.

3. In large nonstick skillet, heat oil and red pepper over medium-high heat until hot. Add beef (half at a time) and stir-fry 1 to 2 minutes or until outside surface is no longer pink. (Do not overcook.) Add sauce, carrot and green onions; cook and stir until sauce is thickened and bubbly.

4. To assemble, spoon small amount of beef mixture in center of each lettuce leaf and fold over to close.

Makes 4 servings (serving size: 4 filled lettuce packets).

Nutritional Information Per Serving

Calories:	238	Protein (g):	29
Calories from total fat: 71		Carbohydrate (g):	12
(Calories from fat in beef: 38)		Cholesterol (mg):	71
Fat (g):	8	Sodium (mg):	644

Step 1. **Cut steak lengthwise in half.**

Step 2. **Cut crosswise into thin strips.**

QUICK & EASY BEEF QUESADILLAS

Crisp outside, brimming with thinly sliced roast beef, salsa and cheese, quesadillas make a quick supper or great halftime snack for sports fans. Serve with additional salsa.

Total preparation and cooking time: 20 minutes

- ½ pound thinly sliced deli roast beef
- ½ cup finely chopped onion
- ½ cup finely chopped green bell pepper
- ½ cup prepared medium salsa
- 1 cup shredded Co-Jack cheese
- 8 flour tortillas (each about 8 inches)
- Vegetable cooking spray

1. Heat oven to 400°. In small microwave-safe bowl, combine onion and bell pepper. Cover, venting one corner, and microwave at high 2 to 3 minutes. Stir in salsa; reserve.

2. Sprinkle 2 tablespoons cheese evenly on each tortilla; arrange deli roast beef over cheese and top with 1 tablespoon salsa mixture. Fold tortillas over to close.

3. Lightly spray two baking sheets with cooking spray. Place four quesadillas on each baking sheet. Lightly spray tops with cooking spray. Bake in 400° oven 10 minutes or until lightly browned.

4. Serve with remaining salsa mixture.

Makes 8 quesadillas (serving size: 1 quesadilla).

Nutritional Information Per Quesadilla

Calories:	218	Protein (g):	14
Calories from total fat: 80		Carbohydrate (g):	20
(Calories from fat in beef: 18)		Cholesterol (mg):	36
Fat (g):	9	Sodium (mg):	349

HARVEST-THYME BEEF SANDWICHES

An easy carrot, turnip and green onion relish flavored with thyme, is layered on toasted rye bread along with thin strips of sirloin.

Total preparation and cooking time: 25 minutes

    1–pound boneless beef top sirloin steak, cut ¾ inch thick
¼ teaspoon salt
¼ teaspoon pepper
8 large oval slices rye **or** sourdough bread, toasted
    Lettuce

Relish
1 cup shredded carrot
1 cup shredded turnip
3 tablespoons sliced green onions
2 tablespoons prepared fat-free Italian dressing
¼ teaspoon dried thyme leaves

1. Heat large nonstick skillet over medium heat until hot. Place beef steak in skillet; cook 10 to 13 minutes for rare to medium doneness, turning once. Season with salt and pepper.

2. Meanwhile in medium bowl, combine relish ingredients; mix well.

3. Line 4 slices of toasted bread with lettuce; spoon equal amount of relish over lettuce. Trim fat from steak. Carve steak crosswise into thin slices. Arrange beef over relish; close sandwiches with remaining toasted bread.

Makes 4 servings (serving size: 1 sandwich).

Nutritional Information Per Serving

Calories:	363	Protein (g):	33
Calories from total fat: 63		Carbohydrate (g):	43
(Calories from fat in beef: 55)		Cholesterol (mg):	76
Fat (g):	7	Sodium (mg):	727

HERBED BURGERS WITH COOL CUCUMBER SAUCE

Burgers with a Mediterranean twist! Aromatic pepper-herb-seasoned ground beef patties cook in a skillet on the stove top in less than 10 minutes. Serve in pita bread with tangy yogurt-cucumber sauce.

Total preparation and cooking time: 20 minutes

- 1 pound lean ground beef
- 1½ teaspoons Pepper-Herb Mix (recipe follows)
  Salt (optional)
- 1 medium tomato, cut into 8 thin slices
- 4 whole pita pocket breads, top ⅓ cut off, warmed

Cucumber Sauce
- ½ cup nonfat plain yogurt
- ⅓ cup chopped cucumber
- ½ teaspoon Pepper-Herb Mix
- ¼ teaspoon salt

1. In small bowl, combine sauce ingredients; mix well. Set aside.

2. Shape ground beef into four ½-inch thick patties. Sprinkle 1½ teaspoons herb mix over both sides of patties.

3. Meanwhile heat large nonstick skillet over medium heat until hot. Place patties in skillet; cook 7 to 8 minutes or until no longer pink and juices run clear, turning once. Season with salt, if desired.

4. Place burger and 2 tomato slices in each pita. Serve with cucumber sauce.

Makes 4 servings (serving size: 1 sandwich).

Nutritional Information Per Serving

Calories:	342	Protein (g):	29
Calories from total fat: 92		Carbohydrate (g):	34
(Calories from fat in beef: 82)		Cholesterol (mg):	70
Fat (g):	10	Sodium (mg):	536

Pepper-Herb Mix

Preparation time: 5 minutes

    2 tablespoons dried basil leaves
    1 tablespoon lemon pepper
    1 tablespoon onion powder
    1 tablespoon dried oregano leaves
  1½ teaspoons rubbed sage

1. Combine all ingredients. Cover and store in airtight container. Shake before using to blend.

Makes about ⅓ cup.

BEEF & BEAN BURRITOS

Quicker than the fast food shop! Simmer lean ground beef and Spicy Seasoning Mix 10 minutes, then combine with convenient canned pinto beans. Spoon into tortillas and serve with fresh vegetable accompaniments.

Total preparation and cooking time: 25 minutes

    1 pound lean ground beef
    1 medium onion, chopped
    1 tablespoon Spicy Seasoning Mix (see page 39)
    ½ teaspoon salt
    1 can (8 ounces) tomato sauce
    1 can (15 ounces) pinto beans, drained, mashed
    8 flour tortillas (each about 8 inches), warmed
       Thinly sliced lettuce, chopped tomatoes and
       sliced green onions (optional)

1. In large nonstick skillet, brown ground beef and onion over medium heat 8 to 10 minutes or until beef is no longer pink, breaking up into ¾-inch crumbles. Pour off drippings.

2. Sprinkle seasoning mix and salt over beef. Stir in tomato sauce. Simmer 10 minutes, stirring occasionally. Stir in beans; heat through.

3. To assemble, spoon equal amount of beef mixture in center of each tortilla. Add lettuce, tomatoes and green onions, if desired. Fold bottom edge up over filling. Fold right and left sides to center, overlapping edges.

Makes 8 burritos (serving size 1 burrito).

Nutritional Information Per Burrito

Calories:	288	Protein (g):	18
Calories from total fat: 74		Carbohydrate (g):	37
(Calories from fat in beef: 41)		Cholesterol (mg):	35
Fat (g):	8	Sodium (mg):	543

OPEN-FACE ROAST BEEF & CRUNCHY VEGETABLES

The sweetness of mango chutney paired with the sharp flavor of horseradish tastes great in this hearty roast beef sandwich on rye. Cucumber is a cooling complement. Be sure to use horseradish sauce, not grated horseradish; the sauce has a milder flavor. (See photograph)

Preparation time: 15 minutes

¾ pound thinly sliced deli roast beef
4 large slices dark rye bread
½ medium cucumber, very thinly sliced
½ small red onion, very thinly sliced
1 tablespoon snipped chives

Sauce
⅓ cup mild horseradish sauce
1 tablespoon chopped Major Grey chutney
2 teaspoons low-fat milk

1. In small bowl, combine sauce ingredients.

2. Spread one side of each bread slice with 2 teaspoons sauce. Top with equal amounts of cucumber, onion and beef. Spoon remaining sauce evenly over beef; sprinkle with chives.

Makes 4 servings (serving size: 1 sandwich).

Nutritional Information Per Serving

Calories:	246	Protein (g):	27
Calories from total fat: 57		Carbohydrate (g):	19
(Calories from fat in beef: 53)		Cholesterol (mg):	69
Fat (g):	6	Sodium (mg):	253

6.
MAKE-AHEAD
"DIVIDEND" DINNERS

F ast, fresh and flavorful "dividend" dinners reward the cook who plans ahead. Dividend dinners can be made in one of two ways. The first is to reserve a few of the ingredients from one recipe to use in a second meal. For example, when preparing Sesame Ginger Grilled Sirloin, you reserve a portion of the grilled steak and peppers along with some of the marinade. The following night these ingredients become the foundation of a main dish salad.

Another option is to do double or triple batch cooking. Triple Batch Beef is an example. Tender cubes of cooked beef, onions and broth are frozen in recipe-size portions for later use in a stew, soup or chili.

Since most of the second meals suggested in this chapter utilize basic ingredients, be sure to keep the pantry, refrigerator and freezer stocked with staples such as salsa, canned beans, frozen vegetables, quick-cooking barley, pasta, prepared spaghetti sauce and shredded cheese.

TRIPLE BATCH BEEF

This basic cooked beef mixture, seasoned with onion and garlic, will provide a flavorful head start for a collection of fast weeknight meals when frozen in recipe-size portions. To be sure the beef is defrosted and ready to use, place in the refrigerator the night before you plan to use it.

Total preparation and cooking time: 2½ hours

4½–pound boneless beef chuck shoulder, arm **or**
     blade pot roast
3 tablespoons vegetable oil
1 teaspoon salt
½ teaspoon pepper
2 medium onions, coarsely chopped
4 cloves garlic, crushed
1½ cups water

1. Trim fat from beef. Cut beef into ¾-inch pieces. In Dutch oven, heat oil over medium heat until hot. Add beef (¼ at a time) and brown evenly, stirring occasionally. Remove beef from pan; season with salt and pepper.

2. In same pan, add onions and garlic; cook and stir until onions are lightly browned. Pour off drippings. Return beef to pan; add water. Bring to a boil; reduce heat to low. Cover tightly and simmer 1½ to 2 hours or until beef is tender.

3. Place about 2 cups beef mixture into each of three 1-quart freezer containers. Cover tightly and freeze. Use beef mixture to prepare Weeknight Beef Stew, 20-Minute Beef Chili and Quick & Easy Beef Barley Soup (see pages 91 to 93).

Makes 6 cups cooked beef.

20-MINUTE BEEF CHILI

A chili that's six-ingredient-quick? Yes, with cooked beef, canned beans, salsa and a few other pantry staples.

Total preparation and cooking time: 20 minutes

- 1 container (2 cups) Triple Batch Beef, defrosted (see page 90)
- 1 jar (8 ounces) mild salsa
- 1 tablespoon chili powder
- 1 can (15 ounces) kidney beans, drained, rinsed
- ½ cup shredded Cheddar cheese
- ¼ cup sliced green onions

1. In medium saucepan, combine beef mixture, salsa and chili powder. Bring to a boil; reduce heat to low. Cover tightly and simmer 10 minutes. Stir in beans; heat through. Serve with cheese and green onions.

Makes 4 servings (serving size: ¼ of recipe).

Nutritional Information Per Serving

Calories:	389	Protein (g):	38
Calories from total fat: 142		Carbohydrate (g):	22
(Calories from fat in beef: 63)		Cholesterol (mg):	101
Fat (g):	16	Sodium (mg):	726

WEEKNIGHT BEEF STEW

The use of pantry ingredients and cooked beef make this beefy stew extra-quick. Just add a fresh fruit salad and crusty rolls for a complete dinner.

Total preparation and cooking time: 20 minutes

- 1 container (2 cups) Triple Batch Beef, defrosted (see page 90)
- 2 medium red potatoes, cut into ¼-inch thick slices
- ⅔ cup water
- 1 teaspoon dried oregano leaves
- ½ teaspoon salt
- 1 cup frozen peas
- 2 teaspoons cornstarch, dissolved in 1 tablespoon fresh lemon juice

1. In medium saucepan, combine beef mixture, potatoes, water, oregano and salt. Bring to a boil; reduce heat to low. Cover tightly and simmer 10 to 12 minutes or until potatoes are tender. Stir in peas; heat through. Add cornstarch mixture; cook and stir 1 minute or until sauce is thickened and bubbly.

Makes 4 servings (serving size: ¼ of recipe).

Nutritional Information Per Serving

Calories:	300	Protein (g):	31
Calories from total fat: 96		Carbohydrate (g):	18
(Calories from fat in beef: 63)		Cholesterol (mg):	86
Fat (g):	11	Sodium (mg):	547

QUICK & EASY BEEF BARLEY SOUP

A steaming bowl of homemade soup can be on the table in almost the time it takes to open a can. Be sure to buy the quick-cooking barley for this recipe. No green beans on hand? Use frozen peas or broccoli florets.

Total preparation and cooking time: 20 minutes

- 1 container (2 cups) Triple Batch Beef, defrosted (see page 90)
- 3 cups water
- 1 cup frozen cut green beans
- 1 cup sliced carrots
- ¼ cup quick-cooking barley
- 1 tablespoon instant beef bouillon granules
- 1 teaspoon dried thyme leaves

1. In large saucepan, combine all ingredients. Bring to a boil; reduce heat to low. Cover tightly and simmer 12 minutes or until barley is tender.

Makes 4 servings (serving size: ¼ of recipe).

Nutritional Information Per Serving

Calories:	286	Protein (g):	31
Calories from total fat: 98		Carbohydrate (g):	16
(Calories from fat in beef: 63)		Cholesterol (mg):	86
Fat (g):	11	Sodium (mg):	508

SAVORY MEATBALLS

A basic meatball recipe is so versatile, and Savory Meatballs offers timesavings as well as reduced fat. By baking the meatballs on a rack, much of the fat is removed. For best results when making meatballs, always handle the ground beef gently and as little as possible. To make ahead, seal cooked meatballs in freezer bags, label and freeze up to one month.

Total preparation and cooking time: 40 to 50 minutes

- 2 pounds lean ground beef
- 1 cup soft bread crumbs
- 2 eggs
- ¼ cup finely chopped onion
- 2 cloves garlic, crushed
- 1 teaspoon salt
- ¼ teaspoon pepper

1. Heat oven to 350°. In large bowl, combine all ingredients, mixing lightly but thoroughly.

For 24 large meatballs:

2. Shape beef mixture into 24 meatballs; place on rack in broiler pan.

3. Bake in 350° oven 25 to 30 minutes or until no longer pink and juices run clear. Use meatballs to prepare Spaghetti & Savory Meatballs and Zesty Meatball Sandwiches (see pages 96 to 97), or freeze up to one month for later use.

For 64 appetizer-size meatballs:

4. Shape beef mixture into 64 (1-inch) meatballs; place on rack in broiler pan.

5. Bake in 350° oven 18 to 20 minutes or until no longer pink and juices run clear. Use meatballs to prepare Mini-Meatballs in Roasted Red Pepper Sauce or Mini-Meatballs in Cranberry-Peach Sauce (see pages 150 to 151), or freeze up to one month for later use.

Cook's Tip: To make soft bread crumbs, place torn bread slices in food processor, fitted with steel blade, or blender container. Cover; process 30 seconds, pulsing on and off, until fine crumbs. One and a half slices will yield 1 cup soft bread crumbs.

SPAGHETTI & SAVORY MEATBALLS

Everyone's favorite pasta dish is weeknight-quick when the meatballs are made ahead. For variety, use spiral-shaped or bow tie pasta and top with grated Romano cheese. Look for garlic bread in your grocer's freezer. (See photograph)

Total preparation and cooking time: 15 minutes

- 12 cooked (½ recipe) large Savory Meatballs (see page 94)
- 8 ounces uncooked spaghetti **or** other pasta
- 1 jar **or** can (26 to 30 ounces) prepared low-fat spaghetti sauce
- 2 tablespoons grated Parmesan cheese (optional)

1. Cook spaghetti according to package directions. Keep warm.

2. Meanwhile in large nonstick skillet, combine meatballs and sauce. Cover and cook over medium-low heat 9 to 11 minutes or until heated through, stirring occasionally.

3. Serve over spaghetti; sprinkle with cheese, if desired.

Makes 6 servings (serving size: ⅙ of recipe).

Nutritional Information Per Serving

Calories:	315	Protein (g):	23
Calories from total fat: 69		Carbohydrate (g):	39
(Calories from fat in beef: 55)		Cholesterol (mg):	82
Fat (g):	8	Sodium (mg):	645

ZESTY MEATBALL SANDWICHES

With a batch or two of meatballs in the freezer, these sandwiches can be ready to serve in minutes. (See photograph)

Total preparation and cooking time: 25 minutes

- 12 cooked (½ recipe) large Savory Meatballs (see page 94)
- 2 tablespoons water
- ½ green bell pepper, cut into thin strips
- ½ onion, cut into thin strips
- 1¼ cups prepared low-fat spaghetti sauce
- ½ teaspoon dried basil leaves
- 4 hoagie rolls (each 5 inches long), split
- ¼ cup shredded part-skim mozzarella cheese (optional)

1. In large nonstick skillet, heat water over medium heat until hot. Add bell pepper and onion; cook and stir 4 minutes or until water is evaporated and vegetables are tender. Reduce heat to medium-low; add meatballs, sauce and basil. Cover and cook 5 to 6 minutes or until heated through, stirring occasionally.

2. Spoon equal amounts of meatball mixture on bottom half of each roll; top with 1 tablespoon cheese, if desired. Close with top half of roll.

Makes 4 servings (serving size: 1 sandwich).

Nutritional Information Per Serving

Calories:	454	Protein (g):	31
Calories from total fat: 131		Carbohydrate (g):	50
(Calories from fat in beef: 82)		Cholesterol (mg):	127
Fat (g):	15	Sodium (mg):	985

◐ Sesame-Ginger Grilled Sirloin

Sirloin is a tender beef cut; it needs only to be marinated for a few minutes to impart the Oriental flavor of the dressing. It's a perfect choice for after-work or weekend entertaining.

Total preparation and cooking time: 30 minutes

2–pound boneless beef top sirloin steak, cut 1½ inches thick

4 red **or** yellow bell peppers, each cut lengthwise in half

Sesame Dressing

3 tablespoons dry sherry

3 tablespoons soy sauce

3 tablespoons white wine vinegar

1 tablespoon sugar

1 tablespoon dark sesame oil

2 teaspoons grated fresh ginger **or** ½ teaspoon ground ginger

2 cloves garlic, crushed

1. In small bowl, whisk together dressing ingredients. Reserve ⅓ cup dressing for Spicy Sesame Beef & Noodles (see page 100); cover and refrigerate.

2. Place beef steak in plastic bag; add remaining dressing, turning to coat. Close bag securely and marinate in refrigerator 15 minutes, turning once.

3. Remove steak from marinade; discard marinade. Place steak and bell peppers on grid over medium coals. Grill 18 to 22 minutes until steak is rare to medium doneness and bell peppers are tender, turning steak and bell peppers once. Trim fat from steak. For Spicy Sesame Beef & Noodles, reserve ½ of cooked steak and 4 pepper halves. Carve remaining steak into slices. Serve with remaining grilled peppers.

Cook's Tip: To check the temperature of coals, cautiously hold the palm of your hand about 4 inches above the coals. Count the number of seconds you can hold your hand in that position before the heat forces you to pull it away. Four seconds for medium coals.

Asian Beef Salad (page 30)

Stir-Fried Sirloin & Spinach with Noodles (page 56)

Lemon Pepper Beef Steak & Potato Wedges (page 46)

Beef & Vegetable Fried Rice (page 48)

Open-Face Roast Beef & Crunchy Vegetables (page 87)

Spicy Orange Beef Lettuce Packets (page 80)

Moo Shu Beef (page 76)

Braised Beef with Vegetables (page 104)
Inset: Simple Italian Beef Manicotti (page 106)

Spaghetti & Savory Meatballs (page 96). Zesty Meatball Sandwiches (page 97)

Lemony Beef & Barley with Sugar Snap Peas (page 116)

T-Bone Steak and Vegetable Dinner for Two (page 120)

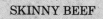

Make-It-Easy Beef Pot Pie (page 110)

Quick Fajitas with Pico de Gallo (page 140)

Perfect Grilled Burgers (page 135). Toppers: Basil Marinated Tomatoes (page 136);
Mango Salsa (page 137); Crisp & Spicy Cabbage Relish (page 138)

Beef Steaks with Grilled Ratatouille & Parmesan Polenta (page 130)

Cheesy Spinach Stuffed Meatloaf (page 168)

Savory Beef Stew with Roasted Vegetables (page 174)

Make-Ahead Beef & Artichoke Appetizers (page 148). Beef & Cheese Pinwheels (page 147). Oriental Beef Kabobs (page 146)

Quick Steak & Vegetable Soup (page 180)

Updated Beef Stroganoff (page 182)

Mini Beef Wellingtons (page 188)

Greek Beef Salad (page 32)

Beef, Tomato & Basil Salad with Garlic Croutons (page 28)

Makes 4 servings (serving size: ¼ of recipe).

Nutritional Information Per Serving

Calories:	193	Protein (g):	26
Calories from total fat: 63		Carbohydrate (g):	4
(Calories from fat in beef: 55)		Cholesterol (mg):	76
Fat (g):	7	Sodium (mg):	250

Spicy Sesame Beef & Noodles

The marinade, bell peppers and beef reserved from Sesame-Ginger Grilled Sirloin are key components of this fast-to-fix main dish salad. Complete the menu with raspberry ice and purchased almond cookies.

Preparation time: 20 minutes

- 12 ounces cooked steak from Sesame-Ginger Grilled Sirloin (see page 98)
- 4 ounces uncooked vermicelli **or** thin spaghetti
- 4 grilled pepper halves (reserved from Sesame-Ginger Grilled Sirloin)
- ½ (6-ounce) package frozen pea pods, defrosted
- ⅓ cup Sesame Dressing (reserved from Sesame-Ginger Grilled Sirloin)
- ¼ teaspoon hot pepper sauce
- 1 teaspoon dark sesame oil
- 2 tablespoons chopped fresh cilantro

1. Cook vermicelli according to package directions.

2. Meanwhile carve beef steak into thin slices. Cut peppers into thin strips. In medium bowl, combine beef, peppers and pea pods. Add dressing and pepper sauce; toss to coat.

3. In large bowl, combine vermicelli and sesame oil; toss to coat. Add beef mixture and cilantro; mix lightly.

Makes 4 servings (serving size: 1¾ cups).

Nutritional Information Per Serving

Calories:	345	Protein (g):	31
Calories from total fat: 93		Carbohydrate (g):	29
(Calories from fat in beef: 55)		Cholesterol (mg):	76
Fat (g):	10	Sodium (mg):	640

TEX-MEX BEEF ROAST

A seasoning rub and salsa added to the cooking liquid subtly flavor this beef roast. Serve thin slices of roast with herb seasoned rice and steamed zucchini. Reserve a portion of the flavorful cooking liquid and sliced beef to make soup for another meal.

Total preparation and cooking time: 45 minutes

2–pound beef eye round **or** tenderloin roast
1 tablespoon Spicy Seasoning Mix (see page 39)
½ teaspoon salt
2 tablespoons vegetable oil
1¼ cups prepared medium salsa
1 can (10½ ounces) beef consommé
1 bay leaf
Water
Salsa

1. Combine seasoning mix and salt; press evenly into surface of beef roast. In Dutch oven, heat oil over medium heat until hot. Add roast; brown evenly. Pour off drippings. Add 1¼ cups salsa, consommé, bay leaf and enough water (about 7 cups) just to cover roast. Bring to a boil; reduce heat to medium-low. Cover tightly and simmer 30 minutes (20 minutes for tenderloin roast) for rare doneness. (Do not overcook.)

2. Remove roast to serving platter. Cover tightly with plastic wrap or aluminum foil and let stand 10 minutes before carving. For Beef & Tortilla Soup (see page 102), reserve ½ of beef and 4 cups cooking liquid.

3. Carve roast into thin slices; serve with salsa.

Makes 4 servings (serving size: ¼ of recipe).

Nutritional Information Per Serving

Calories:	206	Protein (g):	26
Calories from total fat: 69		Carbohydrate (g):	5
(Calories from fat in beef: 38)		Cholesterol (mg):	59
Fat (g):	8	Sodium (mg):	788

BEEF & TORTILLA SOUP

The liquid reserved from Tex-Mex Beef Roast adds robust flavor to this beef soup, brimming with classic Mexican flavors. Instead of frying the tortilla strips, try baking instead. They're crisp and flavorful without added fat. A jicama-orange salad and cinnamon ice cream round out the menu.

Total preparation and cooking time: 20 minutes

12 ounces thinly sliced cooked beef eye round **or** tenderloin roast from Tex-Mex Beef Roast (see page 101)
2 corn tortillas
4 cups cooking liquid (reserved from Tex-Mex Beef Roast)
½ cup chopped tomato
½ cup thinly sliced zucchini
2 tablespoons chopped fresh cilantro
2 tablespoons chopped onion

1. Heat oven to 400°. Lightly sprinkle water on both sides of tortillas; cut each tortilla in half and then crosswise into ¼-inch wide strips. Spread in single layer on 15 × 10-inch jelly roll pan. Bake in 400° oven 5 to 7 minutes or until crisp. Set aside.

2. Meanwhile in 2-quart saucepan, bring cooking liquid to a boil.

3. Cut beef roast into ½-inch wide strips. Place equal amounts of tortilla strips and beef in 4 individual soup bowls. Ladle 1 cup hot liquid into each bowl. Top with equal amounts of tomato, zucchini, cilantro and onion; serve immediately.

Cook's Tip: One large (about 10 inches) flour tortilla may be substituted for 2 corn tortillas. Cut tortilla in half and then crosswise into ¼-inch wide strips. Bake as directed above.

Makes 4 servings (serving size: 1½ cups).

Nutritional Information Per Serving

Calories:	249	Protein (g):	28
Calories from total fat: 70		Carbohydrate (g):	14
(Calories from fat in beef: 38)		Cholesterol (mg):	59
Fat (g):	8	Sodium (mg):	692

BRAISED BEEF WITH VEGETABLES

Less tender beef cuts like pot roast need to simmer over low heat in a tightly covered pan to ensure fork tenderness. This richly flavored roast is delicious served with vegetables for one meal. Reserve a portion of the roast and cooking liquid to make a second, different meal. (See photograph)

Total preparation and cooking time: 2½ hours

 3 to 3½–pound boneless beef chuck arm pot roast
  1 clove garlic, crushed
  1 teaspoon dried oregano leaves
  ½ teaspoon lemon pepper
  ½ teaspoon salt
  1 tablespoon vegetable oil
  ¾ cup water
  2 medium carrots
  2 medium parsnips
  8 small new red potatoes, cut in half
  2 small leeks, cut into 1½-inch pieces
  2 teaspoons cornstarch, dissolved in 1
   tablespoon water

1. Combine garlic, oregano, lemon pepper and salt; press evenly into surface of beef pot roast. In Dutch oven, heat oil over medium-high heat until hot. Add pot roast; brown evenly. Pour off drippings. Add water. Bring to a boil; reduce heat to low. Cover tightly and simmer 1¾ hours.

2. Meanwhile cut carrots and parsnips crosswise into 2½-inch long pieces. Cut large ends lengthwise in halves or quarters. Add vegetables to pan; cover and continue cooking 30 minutes or until beef and vegetables are tender. Remove beef and vegetables to serving platter; keep warm.

3. Strain cooking liquid; skim off fat. For Simple Italian Beef Manicotti (see page 106), reserve about ½ of pot roast (3 cups shredded beef) and ¼ cup cooking liquid.

4. In same pan, return 1 cup cooking liquid. Bring to a boil over medium-high heat. Add cornstarch mixture; cook and stir 1 minute or until sauce is thickened and bubbly. Serve with pot roast and vegetables.

Cook's Tip: To prepare in oven, use covered, ovenproof pot or roasting pan and cook in 325° oven. Cooking times remain the same.

Makes 4 servings (serving size: ¼ of recipe).

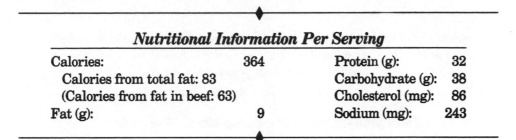

Nutritional Information Per Serving

Calories:	364	Protein (g):	32
Calories from total fat: 83		Carbohydrate (g):	38
(Calories from fat in beef: 63)		Cholesterol (mg):	86
Fat (g):	9	Sodium (mg):	243

Step 1. **Slowly brown meat on all sides in small amount of oil, if desired.**

Step 2. **Pour off drippings.**

Step 3. **Add a small amount of liquid. Season, if desired.**

Step 4. **Cover tightly and simmer on stove top or in oven until meat is tender.**

Step 5. **Add vegetables, if desired, toward end of cooking time.**

Simple Italian Beef Manicotti

Instead of stuffing the manicotti tubes, the flavorful beef filling is rolled inside cooked lasagna noodles. Purchase prepared spaghetti sauce and pre-shredded cheese for additional timesavings. (See photograph)

Total preparation and cooking time: 35 minutes

- 3 cups (12 ounces) shredded cooked beef, reserved from Braised Beef with Vegetables (see page 104)
- 2 to 2½ cups prepared low-fat spaghetti sauce
- ¼ cup cooking liquid (reserved from Braised Beef with Vegetables)
- 2 tablespoons grated Parmesan cheese
- ½ teaspoon dried oregano leaves
- ¼ teaspoon pepper
- 6 cooked lasagna noodles, cut in half
- ½ cup shredded part-skim mozzarella cheese

1. In large bowl, combine beef, ¾ cup sauce, cooking liquid, Parmesan cheese, oregano and pepper. Spread ¼ cup sauce over bottom of 11 × 7-inch microwave-safe baking dish.

2. Spread about ¼ cup beef mixture on each lasagna noodle half. Starting at short end, carefully roll up each noodle jelly-roll fashion. Place seam side down in single layer on bottom of prepared baking dish. Top with remaining sauce; sprinkle with mozzarella cheese.

3. Cover with vented plastic wrap; microwave at high 5 minutes. Reduce power to medium (50% power). Cook 9 to 11 minutes or until filling is hot and cheese is melted, rotating dish ½ turn after 5 minutes. Let stand 2 minutes before serving.

Cook's Tip: For conventional baking, follow recipe as directed above. Do not cover with plastic wrap. Bake in 350° oven 30 to 35 minutes or until filling is hot and cheese is melted.

Makes 4 servings (serving size: 3 manicotti).

Nutritional Information Per Serving

Calories:	409	Protein (g):	39
Calories from total fat: 114		Carbohydrate (g):	33
(Calories from fat in beef: 63)		Cholesterol (mg):	96
Fat (g):	13	Sodium (mg):	743

Step 1. **Braise pot roast in a covered pan until tender.**

Step 2. **Shred cooked meat with two forks.**

7.
FAMILY-STYLE ONE-DISH DINNERS

 he one-dish meals in this chapter feature familiar flavors that will appeal to all ages. Some, such as Italian Beef & Pasta, are ethnic inspired while others are all-American favorites. We've kept the number of ingredients to a minimum, utilized convenience products whenever possible and provided a few surprises along the way.

Aside from easy clean-up, the beauty of a one-dish meal is the fact that few accompaniments are necessary. At most, you might want to add a salad or vegetable and possibly a simple dessert, all of which can be purchased at least partially prepared at the supermarket. All of the following accompaniment ideas are easy to keep on hand.

- crusty French bread, assorted rolls and bagels, whole grain specialty breads, breadsticks
- jarred marinated vegetables (to serve over salad greens)
- a variety of frozen vegetables
- frozen yogurt
- frozen berries

Make-It-Easy Beef Pot Pie

To streamline old-fashioned beef pot pie, tender beef sirloin is paired with a combination of quick-cooking vegetables and a refrigerated biscuit topping. Add a salad or fruit and a glass of milk to complete the menu. (See photograph)

Total preparation and cooking time: 30 minutes

1–pound boneless beef top sirloin steak, cut ¾ inch thick
1 tablespoon vegetable oil
½ pound small mushrooms, quartered
1 medium onion, sliced
1 clove garlic, crushed
¼ cup water
1 jar (12 ounces) beef gravy
1 package (10 ounces) frozen peas and carrots
¼ teaspoon dried thyme leaves
1 small can (4½ ounces) refrigerated buttermilk flavor biscuits

1. Heat oven to 400°. Trim fat from steak. Cut steak lengthwise in half and then crosswise into ¼-inch thick strips. In large ovenproof skillet, heat oil over medium-high heat until hot. Add beef (half at a time) and stir-fry 1 to 2 minutes or until outside surface is no longer pink. (Do not overcook.) Remove from skillet with slotted spoon; set aside.

2. In same skillet, add mushrooms, onion, garlic and water. Cook and stir 3 minutes or until onion is tender. Stir in gravy, vegetables and thyme. Bring to a boil; remove from heat. Stir in reserved beef. Cut biscuits in half; arrange in a ring on top of beef mixture.

3. Bake in 400° oven 12 to 14 minutes or until biscuit topping is golden brown.

Cook's Tip: If skillet is not ovenproof, transfer beef mixture to 9-inch square baking pan. Top with biscuits and bake as recipe directs.

Makes 6 servings (serving size: ⅛ of recipe).

Nutritional Information Per Serving

Calories:	253	Protein (g):	23
Calories from total fat: 80		Carbohydrate (g):	21
(Calories from fat in beef: 37)		Cholesterol (mg):	52
Fat (g):	9	Sodium (mg):	576

Step 1. **Trim fat from steak.**

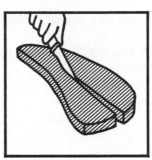

Step 2. **Cut steak lengthwise in half.**

Step 3. **Cut crosswise into thin strips.**

30-Minute Beef Paprikash

Paprika, sauerkraut, sour cream and caraway seeds lend Old World flavor to this single-skillet entree. Traditional noodles cook along with the paprikash—no need to precook them.

Total preparation and cooking time: 30 minutes

            1–pound boneless beef top sirloin steak, cut
                1 inch thick
       1   tablespoon vegetable oil
       2   medium onions, sliced
       1   package (16 ounces) sauerkraut, rinsed,
                drained
       1   tablespoon paprika
       ¼   cup water
       1   can (13¾ to 14½ ounces) ready-to-serve beef
                broth
       ½   cup water
       ¼   cup tomato paste (half of 6-ounce can)
       ½   teaspoon caraway seed
  ⅛ to ¼   teaspoon ground red pepper
      3½   cups uncooked medium noodles
            Chopped fresh parsley
       ¼   cup dairy sour half-and-half

1. Trim fat from beef steak. Cut beef into 1-inch pieces and then cut each in half. In large skillet or Dutch oven, heat oil over medium-high heat until hot. Add beef (half at a time) and stir-fry 1½ to 2 minutes or until outside surface is no longer pink. Remove from skillet with slotted spoon; set aside.

2. In same skillet, add onions, sauerkraut, paprika and ¼ cup water. Cook and stir until onions are tender, about 3 minutes. Stir in broth, ½ cup water, tomato paste, caraway seed, red pepper and noodles, stirring to separate noodles. Bring to a boil; reduce heat to medium. Cover tightly and simmer 10 minutes or until noodles are tender.

3. Remove from heat; return beef to skillet. Cover and let stand 1 minute. Sprinkle with parsley; serve with sour half-and-half.

Makes 5 servings (serving size: 1½ cups).

Nutritional Information Per Serving

Calories:	319	Protein (g):	27
Calories from total fat: 97		Carbohydrate (g):	28
(Calories from fat in beef: 44)		Cholesterol (mg):	90
Fat (g):	11	Sodium (mg):	748

Italian Beef & Pasta

Recipe-ready canned beef broth and tomatoes streamline the preparation of this sure-to-be-favorite main dish. Don't forget slices of crusty Italian bread to dip into the savory sauce.

Total preparation and cooking time: 45 minutes

- 1–pound boneless beef top sirloin steak, cut ½ inch thick
- 1 tablespoon vegetable oil
- 1 medium onion, chopped
- 1 large clove garlic, crushed
- 1 teaspoon Italian seasoning
- 1 can (13¾ to 14½ ounces) ready-to-serve beef broth
- 1 can (14½ ounces) Italian-style diced tomatoes, undrained
- ¼ cup dry red wine
- ½ pound small mushrooms, halved
- 1½ cups uncooked mostaccioli pasta
- 2 tablespoons grated Parmesan cheese
- 1 tablespoon chopped fresh parsley

1. Trim fat from beef steak. Cut steak lengthwise in half and then crosswise into ¼-inch thick strips. In Dutch oven, heat oil over medium-high heat until hot. Add beef (half at a time) and stir-fry 1 to 2 minutes or until outside surface is no longer pink. (Do not overcook.) Remove from pan with slotted spoon; set aside.

2. In same pan, add onion, garlic, Italian seasoning and a few tablespoons of the beef broth. Cook and stir 2 minutes or until tender. Add remaining broth, tomatoes, wine, mushrooms and mostaccioli, stirring to separate pasta. Bring to a boil; reduce heat to medium. Cover tightly and cook 25 to 30 minutes or until pasta is tender. Remove from heat; return beef to pan. (Mixture will be saucy.) Cover and let stand a few minutes. Sprinkle with cheese and parsley before serving.

Makes 4 servings (serving size: 1¾ cups).

Nutritional Information Per Serving

Calories:	391	Protein (g):	35
Calories from total fat: 103		Carbohydrate (g):	34
(Calories from fat in beef: 55)		Cholesterol (mg):	78
Fat (g):	11	Sodium (mg):	772

Lemony Beef & Barley with Sugar Snap Peas

Pairing beef with fresh vegetables and whole grains such as barley makes good nutritional sense. Check the label—quick barley is ready to serve in about 15 minutes while medium pearled barley requires up to an hour to cook. (See photograph)

Total preparation and cooking time: 30 minutes

- 1 pound lean ground beef
- ½ pound mushrooms, sliced
- 1 medium onion, chopped
- 1 large carrot, thinly sliced
- 1 clove garlic, crushed
- 1 can (13¾ to 14½ ounces) ready-to-serve beef broth
- ½ cup quick-cooking barley
- ½ teaspoon salt
- ¼ teaspoon pepper
- 1 package (8 ounces) frozen sugar snap peas, defrosted
- ¼ cup chopped fresh parsley
- 1 teaspoon grated lemon peel

1. In large nonstick skillet, cook and stir ground beef, mushrooms, onion, carrot and garlic over medium heat 8 to 10 minutes or until beef is no longer pink, breaking up into ¾-inch crumbles. Pour off drippings.

2. Stir in broth, barley, salt and pepper. Bring to a boil; reduce heat to medium-low. Cover tightly and simmer 10 minutes.

3. Add peas; continue cooking 2 to 5 minutes or until barley is tender. Stir in parsley and lemon peel.

Makes 4 servings (serving size: 1¾ cups).

Nutritional Information Per Serving

Calories:	259	Protein (g):	27
Calories from total fat: 90		Carbohydrate (g):	17
(Calories from fat in beef: 82)		Cholesterol (mg):	70
Fat (g):	10	Sodium (mg):	665

SPANISH-STYLE BEEF & RICE CASSEROLE

◆

Everyone's favorite Spanish rice gets a main dish treatment with the addition of lean chuck steak.

◆

Total preparation and cooking time: 1¼ hours

1¼ pounds boneless beef chuck shoulder steaks, cut ¾ inch thick
1½ tablespoons olive oil
½ cup chopped green bell pepper
⅓ cup chopped onion
1 clove garlic, crushed
¾ cup uncooked regular long grain rice
2 teaspoons chili powder
¾ teaspoon salt
⅛ teaspoon pepper
1 can (14½ ounces) Mexican-style diced tomatoes, undrained
¾ cup frozen peas, defrosted

1. Heat oven to 350°. Trim fat from beef steaks. Cut steaks lengthwise in half and then crosswise into ¼-inch thick strips.

2. In ovenproof Dutch oven, heat oil over medium-high heat until hot. Add beef, bell pepper, onion and garlic (half at a time) and stir-fry 2 to 3 minutes or until outside surface of beef is no longer pink. Stir in rice, chili powder, salt and pepper.

3. In 2-cup glass measure, add tomatoes and enough water to measure 2 cups; add to beef mixture. Bake in 350° oven, tightly covered, 50 minutes or until beef and rice are tender.

4. Remove from oven; stir in peas.

Makes 4 servings (serving size: ¼ of recipe).

◆

Nutritional Information Per Serving

Calories:	416	Protein (g):	33
Calories from total fat: 116		Carbohydrate (g):	41
(Calories from fat in beef: 63)		Cholesterol (mg):	86
Fat (g):	13	Sodium (mg):	687

BEEF TAMALE PIE

This family-pleasing main dish offers three easy options for the beef. Use deli roast beef, cooked beef reserved from another recipe, or browned and drained ground beef. Add a salad and fresh fruit for dessert.

Total preparation and cooking time: 45 minutes

Filling

2½ cups (¾ pound) cooked lean beef, cut into ½-inch pieces

1 can (15¾ ounces) mild chili beans in chili sauce

1 can (4 ounces) chopped green chilies

¼ cup sliced green onions

¼ teaspoon ground cumin

¼ teaspoon pepper

Cornmeal Base

1 package (8½ ounces) corn muffin mix

1 cup cold water

Topping (optional)

½ cup shredded Cheddar cheese

1. Heat oven to 425°. In medium bowl, combine filling ingredients; mix well. Set aside.

2. In medium bowl, combine cornmeal base ingredients; mix well. (Mixture will be very thin.) Pour batter into greased 9-inch square pan. Spoon beef mixture into center of batter, leaving 1-inch border.

3. Bake in 425° oven 30 minutes or until cornmeal portion is lightly browned and begins to pull away from edges.

4. Remove from oven; sprinkle with cheese, if desired. Let stand 5 minutes before serving.

Makes 8 servings (serving size: ⅛ of recipe).

Nutritional Information Per Serving

Calories:	288	Protein (g):	18
Calories from total fat: 102		Carbohydrate (g):	29
(Calories from fat in beef: 38)		Cholesterol (mg):	61
Fat (g):	11	Sodium (mg):	748

T-Bone Steak & Vegetable Dinner for Two

T-bone steak and a trio of seasoned vegetables star in a special, but easy, broiler meal sized just for two. (See photograph)

Total preparation and cooking time: 20 minutes

- 1–pound beef T-bone **or** Porterhouse steak, cut 1 inch thick
- 1 large potato
- 2 teaspoons olive oil
- ½ teaspoon Italian seasoning
- 1 medium yellow squash, cut lengthwise in half
- 1 small red bell pepper, cut into 6 wedges
- 2 tablespoons grated Parmesan cheese
  Salt and pepper

1. Pierce potato with fork. Microwave at high 3 minutes. Cool slightly; cut lengthwise into 4 wedges.

2. Meanwhile combine oil and Italian seasoning; brush on cut sides of vegetables. Sprinkle with cheese.

3. Place beef steak and vegetables on rack in broiler pan so surface of meat is 3 to 4 inches from heat. Broil steak and vegetables 10 to 15 minutes until steak is rare to medium doneness and vegetables are tender, turning steak and vegetables once. Season steak with salt and pepper, as desired.

4. Trim fat from steak. Remove bone; carve steak crosswise into slices. Serve with vegetables.

Makes 2 servings (serving size: ½ of recipe).

Nutritional Information Per Serving

Calories:	363	Protein (g):	30
Calories from total fat: 140		Carbohydrate (g):	26
(Calories from fat in beef: 79)		Cholesterol (mg):	73
Fat (g):	16	Sodium (mg):	714

Step 1. **Hold steak steady with fork. Use tip of knife to cut closely around bone. Remove bone.**

Step 2. **Carve across steak into strips.**

MEXI-CHILI MAC

Pantry ingredients and one-pan preparation are key to this weeknight family meal. Add the uncooked macaroni to the beef mixture—it cooks during the 15-minute simmering.

Total preparation and cooking time: 30 minutes

- 1 pound lean ground beef
- ½ cup chopped green bell pepper
- ¼ cup chopped onion
- 1 clove garlic, crushed
- 1 can (14½ ounces) Mexican-style diced tomatoes, undrained
- 1 can (8 ounces) tomato sauce
- ¾ cup water
- ¾ cup uncooked elbow macaroni
- 2 teaspoons Spicy Seasoning Mix (see page 39)
- ½ teaspoon salt (optional)

1. In 3-quart saucepan, brown ground beef, bell pepper, onion and garlic over medium heat 8 to 10 minutes or until beef is no longer pink, breaking up into ¾-inch crumbles. Pour off drippings.

2. Stir in remaining ingredients. Bring to a boil; reduce heat to low. Cover tightly and simmer 15 minutes. Remove from heat; cover and let stand 5 minutes before serving.

Makes 4 servings (serving size: 1½ cups).

Nutritional Information Per Serving

Calories:	298	Protein (g):	26
Calories from total fat: 90		Carbohydrate (g):	28
(Calories from fat in beef: 82)		Cholesterol (mg):	70
Fat (g):	10	Sodium (mg):	605

8.

GREAT GRILLED BEEF

 rilling has become a year round favorite way to cook. And no wonder! The complete meal can be cooked on the grill. Many vegetables grill perfectly alongside the beef. Breads, too!

Recipes in this chapter feature quick-cooking beef cuts such as steaks, kabobs and burgers that cook directly over medium temperature coals on an open or covered grill. If you're using a covered grill, foods will cook more quickly than on an open grill. The grilling times provided for these recipes are based on open grill cookery. For perfect grilled beef, follow these easy steps:

1. Cook all beef cuts at medium temperature to ensure that the inside is cooked to the desired doneness without overcooking the outside. Allow about 30 to 45 minutes after lighting charcoal briquets for them to reach medium temperature. At medium, coals should be covered with a layer of gray ash and no longer flaming.

2. To determine the temperature of the coals, cautiously hold your hand 4 inches above the coals. Count the number of seconds before the heat forces you to pull it away: 4 seconds for medium coals.

3. Watch foods carefully during grilling. Grilling times can vary with the position of the grill, weather and temperature of the coals.

Steaks & Summer Squash with Tomato-Cheese Bread

It's a meal on the grill, perfect for entertaining! Zucchini and yellow squash cook with the steak. Grilled French bread topped with tomato slices and mozzarella round out the meal.

Total preparation and cooking time: 25 minutes

- 3 boneless beef top loin **or** 2 Porterhouse steaks, cut 1 inch thick
- 3 zucchini **or** yellow squash, cut lengthwise in half
  Olive oil
  Salt and pepper (optional)

Tomato-Cheese Bread
- 1 loaf French bread (approx. 12 inches long)
- 1 tablespoon olive oil
- 1 large clove garlic, crushed
- 2 small tomatoes, each cut into 6 thin slices
- ¼ teaspoon salt
- ⅛ teaspoon pepper
- ¼ cup shredded part-skim mozzarella cheese
- 2 tablespoons thinly sliced fresh basil

1. Lightly brush squash with oil. Place beef steaks and squash on grid over medium coals. Grill top loin steaks 9 to 12 minutes (Porterhouse steaks 10 to 14 minutes) for rare to medium doneness, turning once. Season with salt and pepper, if desired.

2. Meanwhile cut bread lengthwise in half; brush combined 1 tablespoon oil and garlic evenly on cut sides of bread.

3. About five minutes before steaks are done, place bread, cut side down, on grid with steaks; grill 2 to 3 minutes. Turn bread; place tomatoes on bread halves; season with ¼ teaspoon salt and ⅛ teaspoon pepper. Sprinkle with cheese. Grill, covered, 1 to 3 minutes or until cheese is melted and tomatoes are just heated through. Sprinkle with basil. Cut bread diagonally into slices.

4. Trim fat from steaks. Carve steaks crosswise into thick slices. Serve with grilled squash and bread.

Makes 6 servings (serving size: ⅙ of recipe).

Nutritional Information Per Serving

Calories:	324	Protein (g):	30
Calories from total fat: 122		Carbohydrate (g):	20
(Calories from fat in beef: 72)		Cholesterol (mg):	68
Fat (g):	14	Sodium (mg):	386

CURRIED BEEF KABOBS WITH TOMATO COUSCOUS

Beef and curry have a natural affinity for one another. Because sirloin is a tender cut, the beef pieces need to marinate only a few minutes in the curry, pepper and garlic mixture to impart flavor. Seasoned couscous with tomato is a quick accompaniment—it's prepared and served in just 10 minutes.

Total preparation and cooking time: 30 minutes

1–pound boneless beef top sirloin steak, cut
   1¼ inches thick
2 small onions, each cut into 6 wedges
   Salt (optional)
1 tablespoon chopped fresh cilantro

Marinade
2 teaspoons vegetable oil
1 large clove garlic, crushed
1 teaspoon curry powder
   Dash ground red pepper

1. Trim fat from beef steak. Cut steak into 1¼-inch pieces. In medium bowl, combine marinade ingredients. Add beef and onions, tossing to coat.

2. Alternately thread beef and onions onto each of four 12-inch metal skewers.

3. Place kabobs on grid over medium coals. Grill 8 to 11 minutes for rare to medium doneness, turning once. Season with salt, if desired. Sprinkle with cilantro.

4. Meanwhile prepare Tomato Couscous. Serve kabobs with couscous.

Tomato Couscous

2 teaspoons vegetable oil
¼ cup slivered almonds
1 large clove garlic, crushed
1 teaspoon curry powder
   Dash ground red pepper
1 cup boiling water
¾ cup couscous
½ teaspoon salt
2 small tomatoes, chopped

1. In small saucepan, heat oil over medium heat until hot. Cook and stir almonds, garlic, curry powder and red pepper 4 to 5 minutes or until almonds are lightly browned.

2. Remove pan from heat; stir in boiling water, couscous and salt. Cover and let stand 5 minutes. Add tomatoes, mixing lightly.

Cook's Tip: Kabobs can also be broiled. Place kabobs on rack in broiler pan so surface of meat is 3 to 4 inches from heat. Broil 9 to 12 minutes, turning occasionally.

Makes 4 servings (serving size: 1 kabob and ¾ cup couscous).

Nutritional Information Per Serving

Calories:	401	Protein (g):	32
Calories from total fat: 134		Carbohydrate (g):	33
(Calories from fat in beef: 55)		Cholesterol (mg):	76
Fat (g):	15	Sodium (mg):	333

GRILLED CHOPPED STEAKS WITH CORN RELISH

Juicy grilled chopped steaks are complemented by tangy Corn Relish. For the relish, use convenient frozen corn or roast fresh corn on the grill.

Total preparation and cooking time: 30 minutes

Chopped Steaks
- 1 pound lean ground beef
- ¼ cup finely chopped onion
- ½ teaspoon ground cumin
- ½ teaspoon salt
- ¼ teaspoon pepper

Corn Relish
- 1 cup frozen corn, defrosted
- ½ cup seeded and chopped tomato
- ½ cup seeded and chopped cucumber
- 3 tablespoons sliced green onions
- 1½ tablespoons cider vinegar
- 2 teaspoons olive oil
- 1 teaspoon sugar
- ½ teaspoon ground cumin
- ¼ teaspoon salt

1. In large bowl, combine chopped steak ingredients, mixing lightly but thoroughly. Shape into four ¾-inch thick patties.

2. Combine Corn Relish ingredients; toss to coat. Set aside.

3. Place patties on grid over medium coals. Grill patties 10 to 11 minutes or until no longer pink and juices run clear, turning once. Serve with Corn Relish.

Cook's Tip: For roasted corn relish, remove silk from 1 ear fresh corn on the cob. Sprinkle with 2 tablespoons water. Pull husk up around corn and twist to close. Place corn on grid over medium coals; cover grill. Grill 15 to 20 minutes or until tender, turning occasionally. Remove husk; cut kernels from cob for use in relish.

Makes 4 servings (serving size: 1 chopped steak and ½ cup Corn Relish).

Nutritional Information Per Serving

Calories:	244	Protein (g):	24
Calories from total fat: 107		Carbohydrate (g):	13
(Calories from fat in beef: 82)		Cholesterol (mg):	70
Fat (g):	12	Sodium (mg):	472

BEEF STEAKS WITH GRILLED RATATOUILLE & PARMESAN POLENTA

It's a complete meal from the grill and a new twist for ratatouille. Traditional ingredients are brushed with seasoned oil, then grilled on a skewer alongside lean steaks and polenta wedges. (See photograph)

Total preparation and cooking time: 50 minutes

- 3 boneless beef top loin steaks, cut 1 inch thick
- 2 medium Japanese eggplants, cut into 1-inch pieces
- 1 medium onion, cut into 1-inch pieces
- 1 medium yellow squash, cut into 1-inch slices
- 1 medium zucchini, cut into 1-inch slices
- 1 small red bell pepper, cut into 1-inch pieces
  Salt and pepper (optional)
  Chopped fresh parsley (optional)

Dressing
- ¼ cup prepared fat-free Italian dressing
- 1 clove garlic, crushed
- ¼ teaspoon pepper

1. Prepare Parmesan Polenta.

2. Meanwhile alternately thread eggplant, onion, yellow squash, zucchini and bell pepper onto four 12-inch metal skewers. In small bowl, whisk together dressing ingredients. Brush lightly on kabobs; reserve remaining dressing.

3. Place beef steaks and vegetable kabobs on grid over medium coals. Grill 9 to 12 minutes until steaks are rare to medium doneness and vegetables are tender, turning steaks once and kabobs occasionally.

4. Trim fat from steaks. Carve steaks crosswise into thick slices. Place on warm platter; season with salt and pepper, if desired.

5. Remove vegetables from skewers to serving bowl. Toss with reserved dressing. Sprinkle with parsley, if desired. Serve steaks with ratatouille and polenta.

Parmesan Polenta

2¾ cups water
¾ cup yellow cornmeal
½ teaspoon salt
½ cup shredded part-skim mozzarella cheese
1 to 2 tablespoons grated Parmesan cheese

1. In 1-quart microwave-safe dish, combine water, cornmeal and salt. Cover; microwave at high 10 to 12 minutes, stirring once. Stir in mozzarella cheese; cover and let stand 2 minutes.

2. Spread cornmeal mixture into lightly oiled 9-inch round pan. Cool slightly. Cover and refrigerate until firm, at least 1 hour or overnight, if desired.

3. Cut into 6 wedges. Grill over medium coals 12 to 15 minutes or until browned and heated through, turning once. Sprinkle with Parmesan cheese.

Makes 6 servings (serving size: ⅙ of recipes).

Nutritional Information Per Serving

Calories:	339	Protein (g):	34
Calories from total fat: 123		Carbohydrate (g):	20
(Calories from fat in beef: 72)		Cholesterol (mg):	78
Fat (g):	14	Sodium (mg):	637

TERIYAKI BEEF KABOBS

Loosely thread the beef, pineapple and colorful peppers onto skewers to ensure even cooking throughout. For convenience, use ready-cut or cored pineapple from the produce section.

Total preparation and cooking time: 35 minutes

1–pound boneless beef top sirloin steak, cut 1¼ inches thick
½ fresh pineapple, peeled, cored, cut into 1-inch pieces
1 small green bell pepper, cut into 1-inch pieces
1 small red bell pepper, cut into 1-inch pieces
2 cups hot cooked rice

Marinade
¼ cup packed light brown sugar
3 tablespoons dry sherry
3 tablespoons soy sauce
2 teaspoons dark sesame oil
2 large cloves garlic, crushed
½ teaspoon ground ginger

1. Trim fat from beef steak. Cut steak into 1¼-inch pieces. In small bowl, combine marinade ingredients. Place beef in plastic bag; add ½ of marinade, turning to coat. Close bag securely and marinate in refrigerator 20 minutes. Reserve remaining marinade.

2. Remove beef from marinade; discard marinade. Alternately thread equal amounts of beef, pineapple and bell peppers onto each of four 12-inch metal skewers.

3. Place kabobs on grid over medium coals. Grill 8 to 11 minutes for rare to medium doneness, turning and brushing with reserved marinade occasionally. Serve with rice.

Makes 4 servings (serving size: 1 kabob and ½ cup rice).

Nutritional Information Per Serving

Calories:	407	Protein (g):	30
Calories from total fat: 76		Carbohydrate (g):	50
(Calories from fat in beef: 55)		Cholesterol (mg):	76
Fat (g):	8	Sodium (mg):	641

MEXICALI BARBECUED STEAKS

Sweet and spicy salsa glazes top loin steaks as they grill.

Total preparation and cooking time: 20 minutes

1 to 1¼ pounds boneless beef top loin **or** rib eye
      steaks, cut 1 inch thick

Glaze
  ½ cup mild **or** medium prepared salsa
  ¼ cup ketchup
  2 tablespoons packed brown sugar
  1 tablespoon Dijon-style mustard

1. In small bowl, combine glaze ingredients; mix until blended. Reserve ¾ cup.

2. Place beef steaks on grid over medium coals. Grill 9 to 12 minutes for rare to medium doneness, turning once. Brush both sides of steaks with remaining glaze during last 3 to 4 minutes of grilling time.

3. Trim fat from steaks. Carve steaks crosswise into thick slices. Serve with reserved glaze.

Makes 4 servings (serving size: ¼ of recipe).

Nutritional Information Per Serving

Calories:	224	Protein (g):	25
Calories from total fat: 74		Carbohydrate (g):	12
(Calories from fat in beef: 72)		Cholesterol (mg):	65
Fat (g):	8	Sodium (mg):	459

HONEY-MUSTARD GLAZED STEAKS WITH GRILLED ONIONS

Seasoned honey-mustard glaze is delicious on both the steak and onions, especially mingled with the subtle smoky flavor imparted by grilling. Serve with a mixed green salad.

Total preparation and cooking time: 30 minutes

4 boneless beef top loin steaks, cut 1 inch thick
2 large onions, cut into ½-inch thick slices

Honey-Mustard Glaze

⅛ cup honey mustard
2 tablespoons water
1 tablespoon fresh rosemary, snipped **or** 1 teaspoon dried rosemary, crushed
1 tablespoon white wine vinegar
1 large clove garlic, crushed
1 teaspoon grated fresh ginger
½ teaspoon coarse grind black pepper

1. In small bowl, combine glaze ingredients; mix well.

2. Place beef steaks and onions on grid over medium coals. Generously brush both sides of steaks and onions with glaze. Grill 9 to 12 minutes until steaks are rare to medium doneness and onions are tender, turning once.

3. Trim fat from steaks. Carve steaks crosswise into thick slices; serve with grilled onions.

Makes 8 servings (serving size: ⅛ of recipe).

Nutritional Information Per Serving

Calories:	203	Protein (g):	25
Calories from total fat: 77		Carbohydrate (g):	5
(Calories from fat in beef: 72)		Cholesterol (mg):	65
Fat (g):	9	Sodium (mg):	185

PERFECT GRILLED BURGERS

The quintessential favorite for outdoor grilling—a thick, juicy burger. Make sure coals are medium temperature so that burgers cook through. (See photograph)

Total preparation and cooking time: 15 minutes

  1½ pounds lean ground beef
      Salt and pepper (optional)
  6 hamburger buns, split

1. Shape ground beef into six ½-inch thick patties.

2. Place patties on grid over medium coals. Grill 7 to 9 minutes or until no longer pink and juices run clear, turning once. Season with salt and pepper, if desired, after turning.

3. Serve grilled burgers on buns with **Basil Marinated Tomatoes, Mango Salsa** or **Crisp & Spicy Cabbage Relish** (see pages 136 to 138), if desired.

Makes 6 servings (serving size: 1 sandwich).

Nutritional Information Per Serving

Calories:	288	Protein (g):	25
Calories from total fat: 102		Carbohydrate (g):	21
(Calories from fat in beef: 82)		Cholesterol (mg):	72
Fat (g):	11	Sodium (mg):	268

BASIL MARINATED TOMATOES

This colorful fresh tomato and basil topping for burgers is destined to become a new favorite. (See photograph)

Preparation time: 10 minutes

6 tomato slices, ¼ inch thick
6 thin red onion slices
1 tablespoon thinly sliced fresh basil
1 tablespoon olive oil
2 teaspoons red wine vinegar
½ teaspoon sugar

1. Place tomato slices in shallow dish; top each with one onion slice.

2. Combine remaining ingredients, mixing until well blended. Pour over tomato and onion. Cover and refrigerate up to 1 hour. Serve with Perfect Grilled Burgers.

Makes 6 servings (serving size: ⅙ of recipe).

Nutritional Information Per Serving

Calories:	28	Protein (g):	0
Calories from total fat: 21		Carbohydrate (g):	2
		Cholesterol (mg):	0
Fat (g):	2	Sodium (mg):	1

Mango Salsa

Salsa with a difference! Sweet, colorful mango is a delicious option instead of tomatoes. Substitute 2 to 3 large ripe nectarines for the mangoes if you like. (See photograph)

Preparation time: 10 minutes

- 2 pounds fresh mangoes, peeled, seeded
- 2 tablespoons chopped green onion
- 1 tablespoon fresh lime juice
- 1 tablespoon chopped fresh cilantro
- 1 serrano **or** jalapeño pepper, seeded, finely chopped

1. Coarsely chop mangoes to make 1½ cups. In medium bowl, combine mangoes with remaining ingredients; mix lightly. Cover and refrigerate. Serve with Perfect Grilled Burgers.

Makes 1½ cups (serving size: ¼ cup).

Nutritional Information Per Serving

Calories:	72	Protein (g):	1
Calories from total fat: 0		Carbohydrate (g):	19
		Cholesterol (mg):	0
Fat (g):	0	Sodium (mg):	3

CRISP & SPICY CABBAGE RELISH

Serve this crispy, spicy cabbage topper over burgers, or double the recipe and serve as a side dish. Pre-shredded cabbage makes preparation a cinch! (See photograph)

Total preparation and cooking time: 10 minutes
Chilling time: 1 hour or overnight, if desired

1½ cups packaged coleslaw mix
¼ cup chopped red onion
¼ cup chopped green **or** red bell pepper

Dressing
1½ teaspoons dark sesame oil
½ to 1 jalapeño pepper, seeded, finely chopped
1 clove garlic, crushed
⅛ to ¼ teaspoon pepper
2 tablespoons sugar
2 tablespoons white wine vinegar

1. In medium bowl, combine coleslaw mix, onion and bell pepper.

2. In small saucepan, heat oil over medium-low heat until hot. Add jalapeño pepper, garlic and pepper; cook and stir 1 minute. Add sugar and vinegar; cook and stir 30 seconds or until sugar is dissolved.

3. Pour hot dressing over cabbage mixture; toss to coat. Cover and refrigerate 1 hour or overnight, if desired. Serve with Perfect Grilled Burgers.

Cook's Tip: Thinly sliced green cabbage may be substituted for packaged coleslaw mix.

Makes 1½ cups (serving size: ¼ cup).

Nutritional Information Per Serving

Calories:	37	Protein (g):	0
Calories from total fat: 11		Carbohydrate (g):	7
		Cholesterol (mg):	0
Fat (g):	1	Sodium (mg):	4

GARLICKY BEEF & SPUDS

Lemon, garlic and pepper flavor this barbecue favorite. Potatoes grill alongside the beef. When cooked rare in the center, the outside edges of the tri-tip roast will be medium to well-done. If you have leftovers, toss strips of beef and potatoes with prepared vinaigrette for an easy main dish salad.

Total preparation and cooking time: 60 minutes

- 1 beef tri-tip (bottom sirloin) roast
- 1 clove garlic, crushed
- ½ teaspoon pepper
- 18 small new potatoes
- Salt (optional)

Marinade
- 3 tablespoons olive oil
- 2 tablespoons fresh lemon juice
- 1 clove garlic, crushed

1. **Combine marinade ingredients. Press combined 1 clove crushed garlic and pepper evenly into surface of beef roast. Place beef in plastic bag; add 2 tablespoons marinade, turning to coat. Close bag securely and marinate in refrigerator 20 minutes, turning once.**

2. **Thread potatoes onto three 12-inch metal skewers; brush with remaining marinade.**

3. **Remove beef from marinade; discard marinade. Place beef and potatoes on grid over medium coals. Grill 30 to 35 minutes until beef is rare to medium doneness and potatoes are tender, turning once. Let stand 10 minutes before carving.**

4. **Trim fat from beef. Carve beef across the grain into slices. Remove potatoes from skewers; serve with beef. Season with salt, if desired.**

Cook's Tip: Recipe may be doubled.

Makes 6 servings (serving size: ⅙ of recipe).

Nutritional Information Per Serving

Calories:	290	Protein (g):	27
Calories from total fat: 95		Carbohydrate (g):	21
(Calories from fat in beef: 74)		Cholesterol (mg):	48
Fat (g):	10	Sodium (mg):	74

QUICK FAJITAS
WITH PICO DE GALLO

Grill traditional fajita accompaniments—bell pepper and onion—alongside the steak. Heat foil-wrapped tortillas on the grill, too—about 5 minutes, turning once. Pico de Gallo (a relish of tomatoes, cilantro, picante sauce and zucchini) garnishes the fajitas. (See photograph)

Total preparation and cooking time: 45 minutes

    1–pound boneless beef top sirloin steak, cut
       ¾ inch thick **or** flank steak
    8 flour tortillas (each about 8 inches), warmed

Marinade
    2 tablespoons fresh lime juice
    2 teaspoons vegetable oil
    2 cloves garlic, crushed

1. Combine marinade ingredients. Place beef steak in plastic bag; add marinade, turning to coat. Close bag securely and marinate in refrigerator 20 to 30 minutes, turning once.

2. Meanwhile prepare Pico de Gallo.

3. Remove steak from marinade; discard marinade. Place steak on grid over medium coals. Grill 12 to 16 minutes for rare to medium doneness, turning once.

4. Trim fat from steak. Carve steak crosswise into slices; serve in tortillas with Pico de Gallo.

Pico de Gallo

½ cup diced zucchini
½ cup seeded, chopped tomato
¼ cup chopped fresh cilantro
¼ cup prepared picante sauce **or** salsa
 1 tablespoon fresh lime juice

1. In medium bowl, combine all ingredients; mix well.

Makes 4 servings (serving size: 2 filled tortillas and ¼ cup Pico de Gallo).

Nutritional Information Per Serving

Calories:	433	Protein (g):	32
Calories from total fat: 116		Carbohydrate (g):	46
(Calories from fat in beef: 55)		Cholesterol (mg):	76
Fat (g):	13	Sodium (mg):	507

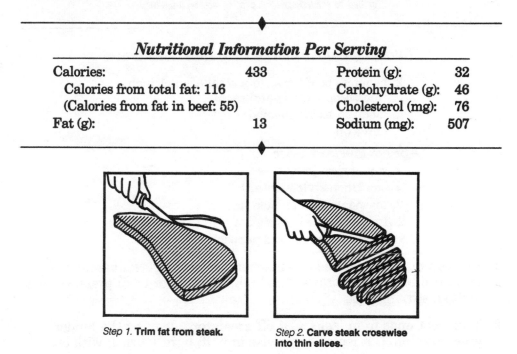

Step 1. **Trim fat from steak.**   Step 2. **Carve steak crosswise into thin slices.**

Apricot-Mustard Glazed Sirloin with Grilled Leeks

A sweet-hot, quick glaze is brushed over sirloin steak as it grills. Mild flavored leeks, grilled to tenderness, are a tasty accompaniment.

Total preparation and cooking time: 30 minutes

2　boneless beef top sirloin steaks, cut 1 inch thick (approx. 1 pound each)
4　medium leeks, cleaned
　　Olive oil

Apricot-Mustard Glaze
⅓　cup apricot preserves
¼　cup Dijon-style mustard
2　teaspoons fresh lemon juice
½　teaspoon dried thyme leaves
⅛　teaspoon ground red pepper

1. In 1-cup microwave-safe glass measure, combine glaze ingredients; mix until blended. Microwave at high 1 minute or until preserves are melted, stirring once.

2. Trim root ends from leeks. Cut off green tops, leaving the tender green portion. Cut leeks lengthwise in half; lightly brush with oil.

3. Place beef steaks and leeks on grid over medium coals. Grill 16 to 20 minutes until steaks are rare to medium doneness and leeks are tender, turning once. Generously brush steaks with glaze during last 5 minutes.

4. Trim fat from steaks. Carve steaks crosswise into slices; serve with leeks.

Makes 8 servings (serving size: ⅛ of recipe).

Nutritional Information Per Serving

Calories:	254	Protein (g):	27
Calories from total fat: 70		Carbohydrate (g):	18
(Calories from fat in beef: 55)		Cholesterol (mg):	76
Fat (g):	8	Sodium (mg):	164

CARNE ASADA

A simple blend of lime juice and Spicy Seasoning Mix adds extra zesty Southwestern flavor to steaks on the grill. Serve with a fresh salsa and flour tortillas warmed on the grill.

Total preparation and cooking time: 30 minutes

- 4 boneless beef top loin **or** rib eye steaks, cut ¾ inch thick (about 2 pounds)
- 2 tablespoons fresh lime juice
- 1 tablespoon Spicy Seasoning Mix (see page 39)
- ½ cup shredded Co-Jack **or** Cheddar cheese

1. Sprinkle both sides of beef steaks with lime juice; sprinkle with seasoning mix.

2. Place steaks on grid over medium coals. Grill 7 to 9 minutes for rare to medium doneness, turning once. Meanwhile prepare Fresh Tomato Salsa.

3. Trim fat from steaks. Cut each steak crosswise in half; top each with equal amounts of cheese and salsa.

Fresh Tomato Salsa

- 2 medium tomatoes, seeded, chopped
- 2 tablespoons thinly sliced green onion
- 1 tablespoon chopped fresh cilantro
- 1 tablespoon fresh lime juice
- 1 jalapeño pepper, seeded, finely chopped
- ¼ teaspoon salt
- ¼ teaspoon pepper

1. In medium bowl, combine all ingredients; mix well.

Makes 8 servings (serving size: ⅛ of recipes).

Nutritional Information Per Serving

Calories:	216	Protein (g):	27
Calories from total fat: 94		Carbohydrate (g):	3
(Calories from fat in beef: 72)		Cholesterol (mg):	71
Fat (g):	10	Sodium (mg):	174

9.

EFFORTLESS ENTERTAINING

 ntertaining can be effortless when you can rely on a collection of great-tasting beef recipes that are simple to prepare and suitable for a variety of year 'round occasions.

Many of the recipes in this chapter feature beef cuts and cooking methods that lend themselves to those times when you need to prepare a special meal in short order, a weeknight birthday celebration, for example. Several of these main dishes include vegetables and a side dish such as pasta; others need little more than a salad and bread to round out the meal.

When the occasion calls for casual entertaining, whether it's halftime fare for football fans or several substantial appetizers instead of a meal, this chapter offers easy, speedy and delicious choices.

ORIENTAL BEEF KABOBS

Purchased hoisin sauce, sesame oil and sherry flavor these appetizer-size kabobs. Make plenty—they will go fast! (See photograph)

Total preparation and cooking time: 25 minutes

1–pound boneless beef top sirloin steak, cut
    1 inch thick
¼ cup hoisin sauce
2 tablespoons dry sherry
2 teaspoons packed light brown sugar
1 teaspoon dark sesame oil
6 green onions, sliced diagonally into 1½-inch
    pieces

1. Soak sixteen 6-inch bamboo skewers in enough water to cover 10 minutes; drain.

2. Meanwhile combine hoisin sauce, sherry, brown sugar and sesame oil; set aside.

3. Trim fat from beef steak. Cut steak crosswise into ¼-inch thick strips. Alternately thread beef, weaving back and forth, and green onion pieces onto skewers.

4. Place kabobs on rack in broiler pan so surface of kabobs is 3 to 4 inches from heat. Brush with half of hoisin mixture. Broil 5 to 6 minutes, turning once, and brushing with remaining hoisin mixture.

Makes 16 appetizers (serving size: 1 kabob).

Nutritional Information Per Appetizer

Calories:	53	Protein (g):	7
Calories from total fat: 17		Carbohydrate (g):	2
(Calories from fat in beef: 14)		Cholesterol (mg):	19
Fat (g):	2	Sodium (mg):	47

BEEF & CHEESE PINWHEELS

This colorful appetizer requires just five ingredients and can be assembled up to six hours before serving. (See photograph)

Preparation time: 20 minutes

12 ounces thinly sliced deli roast beef
 1 package (4 ounces) herb flavored soft
    spreadable cheese
 4 large flour tortillas (each about 10 inches)
 2 cups spinach leaves (about 20 leaves)
 1 jar (7 ounces) roasted red peppers, rinsed,
    drained

1. Spread cheese evenly over one side of each tortilla. Place deli roast
   beef over cheese leaving ½-inch border around edges. Place spinach
   leaves over beef. Arrange peppers down center, over spinach. Roll up
   tightly; wrap in plastic wrap. Refrigerate at least 30 minutes or up to
   6 hours before serving.

2. To serve, cut each roll crosswise into 8 slices; arrange cut side up on
   serving platter.

Makes 32 appetizers (serving size: 1 pinwheel).

Nutritional Information Per Appetizer

Calories:	50	Protein (g):	4
Calories from total fat: 16		Carbohydrate (g):	4
(Calories from fat in beef: 7)		Cholesterol (mg):	10
Fat (g):	2	Sodium (mg):	54

MAKE-AHEAD BEEF & ARTICHOKE APPETIZERS

Pick up the ingredients for these appetizers on your way home from work. They can be assembled in minutes. (See photograph)

Total preparation and cooking time: 30 minutes

- 1 pound deli roast beef, sliced ⅛ inch thick
- ¼ cup prepared fat-free Italian dressing
- 2 cans (14 ounces each) quartered artichoke hearts, drained
- 1 basket cherry tomatoes, cut in half
- 1 can (6 ounces) small pitted ripe olives, drained (optional)
- ¼ cup prepared fat-free Italian dressing

1. Place deli roast beef in utility dish; add ¼ cup dressing, turning to coat.

2. In large bowl, combine artichoke hearts, tomatoes, olives, if desired, and remaining dressing; toss to coat.

3. Remove beef from dressing (one slice at a time); roll up tightly from wide end. Cut into ¾-inch wide pinwheels.

4. To assemble, alternately thread two beef pinwheels, two artichoke pieces, two tomato halves and two olives, if desired, on each of twenty-four 6-inch bamboo skewers. Serve immediately or cover and refrigerate until serving time.

Makes 24 appetizers (serving size: 1 skewer).

Nutritional Information Per Appetizer

Calories:	49	Protein (g):	6
Calories from total fat: 12		Carbohydrate (g):	3
(Calories from fat in beef: 12)		Cholesterol (mg):	15
Fat (g):	1	Sodium (mg):	71

MEXICAN PIZZAS

Quick-to-fix Mexican Pizzas have built-in versatility. You can use tortillas or pita bread for the base and vary the cheese. They'll make great halftime fare for sports fans!

Total preparation and cooking time: 30 minutes

- 1 pound lean ground beef
- 1 medium onion, chopped
- 1 can (8 ounces) tomato sauce
- 2 teaspoons Spicy Seasoning Mix (see page 39)
- ½ teaspoon salt
- 4 flour tortillas (each about 8 inches)
  Vegetable cooking spray
- ¼ cup shredded Monterey Jack cheese
- ¼ cup sliced ripe olives

1. Heat oven to 400°. In large nonstick skillet, brown ground beef and onion over medium heat 8 to 10 minutes or until beef is no longer pink, breaking up into ¾-inch crumbles. Pour off drippings. Stir in tomato sauce, seasoning mix and salt. Simmer 10 minutes, stirring occasionally.

2. Place tortillas on 2 baking sheets; lightly spray tortillas with cooking spray. Bake in 400° oven 3 minutes. Top each tortilla with equal amount of beef mixture; sprinkle each with cheese and olives. Return pizzas to oven. Continue baking 5 minutes.

3. To serve, cut each pizza into 4 wedges.

Cook's Tip: Two 6-inch whole pita pocket breads, split horizontally, may be substituted for flour tortillas. Omit spraying with cooking spray.

Makes 16 appetizers (serving size: 1 wedge).

Nutritional Information Per Appetizer

Calories:	96	Protein (g):	7
Calories from total fat: 37		Carbohydrate (g):	8
(Calories from fat in beef: 21)		Cholesterol (mg):	19
Fat (g):	4	Sodium (mg):	248

MINI-MEATBALLS IN ROASTED RED PEPPER SAUCE

Thyme and white wine flavor the roasted red pepper sauce paired with these cocktail-size meatballs. Look for roasted peppers with the other marinated vegetables in the Italian food section of your supermarket.

Total preparation and cooking time: 30 minutes

- 1 recipe cooked appetizer-size Savory Meatballs (see page 94)
- 1 tablespoon olive oil
- 1 medium onion, finely chopped
- 3 cloves garlic, crushed
- 1 cup ready-to-serve beef broth
- 2 teaspoons cornstarch
- 2 jars (7 ounces each) roasted red peppers, rinsed, drained, finely chopped
- ½ cup dry white wine
- 2 tablespoons tomato paste
- ¾ teaspoon dried thyme leaves

1. In large nonstick skillet, heat oil over medium heat until hot. Add onion and garlic; cook and stir 2 to 3 minutes or until tender.

2. Combine broth and cornstarch; add to skillet with red peppers, wine, tomato paste and thyme. Bring to a boil; reduce heat to medium-low. Simmer 10 to 12 minutes or until slightly thickened, stirring occasionally.

3. Add meatballs to skillet; continue to cook until meatballs are heated through, stirring occasionally.

Makes 64 appetizers (serving size: 1 meatball with sauce).

Nutritional Information Per Appetizer

Calories:	32	Protein (g):	3
Calories from total fat: 14		Carbohydrate (g):	1
(Calories from fat in beef: 10)		Cholesterol (mg):	15
Fat (g):	2	Sodium (mg):	64

Mini-Meatballs in Cranberry-Peach Sauce

Miniature meatballs are tried-and-true appetizer fare. Save time by making the meatballs ahead and freezing. On party day, defrost in the refrigerator and add to the piquant fruit sauce just long enough to heat through.

Total preparation and cooking time: 25 minutes

- 1 recipe cooked appetizer-size Savory Meatballs (see page 94)
- 2 tablespoons finely chopped green onion

Cranberry-Peach Sauce
- 1 can (16 ounces) whole berry cranberry sauce
- 1 can (8 ounces) sliced peaches in light syrup, drained
- ½ cup prepared mild picante sauce **or** salsa
- 2 tablespoons cider vinegar
- ½ teaspoon grated fresh ginger
  Dash ground allspice

1. In food processor, fitted with steel blade, combine cranberry sauce and peaches. Cover; process, pulsing on and off, until finely chopped.

2. In large nonstick skillet, combine fruit mixture and remaining sauce ingredients. Bring to a boil; reduce heat to medium-low. Simmer 5 minutes, stirring occasionally.

3. Add meatballs to skillet; continue to cook until meatballs are heated through, stirring occasionally. Garnish with green onion.

Makes 64 appetizers (serving size: 1 meatball with sauce).

Nutritional Information Per Appetizer

Calories:	38	Protein (g):	3
Calories from total fat: 12		Carbohydrate (g):	4
(Calories from fat in beef: 10)		Cholesterol (mg):	15
Fat (g):	1	Sodium (mg):	64

TENDERLOIN STEAKS WITH PEPPER JELLY SAUCE

A single skillet is all you need to cook the steaks and prepare the sauce for this fast-to-fix main dish ideally suited for weeknight entertaining. Look for jalapeno pepper jelly with the other condiments in your supermarket.

Total preparation and cooking time: 30 minutes

- 4 beef tenderloin steaks **or** 2 boneless top loin steaks, cut 1 inch thick
- ¾ teaspoon garlic salt
- ¾ teaspoon chili powder
- ½ teaspoon coarse grind black pepper
- ¼ teaspoon ground cumin
- ¼ teaspoon dried oregano leaves
  Vegetable cooking spray
- ½ cup ready-to-serve beef broth
- ¼ cup balsamic **or** red wine vinegar
- 2 tablespoons jalapeño pepper jelly

1. Combine garlic salt, chili powder, pepper, cumin and oregano; press evenly into both sides of each beef steak. Spray large nonstick skillet with cooking spray; heat over medium heat until hot. Place steaks in skillet; cook 9 to 11 minutes for rare to medium doneness, turning once. Trim fat from steaks. (Cut top loin steaks crosswise in half.) Transfer steaks to serving platter; keep warm.

2. Add broth, vinegar and jelly to skillet; cook and stir until browned bits attached to skillet are dissolved and sauce thickens slightly. Spoon sauce over steaks.

Makes 4 servings (serving size: ¼ of recipe).

Nutritional Information Per Serving

Calories:	213	Protein (g):	24
Calories from total fat: 78		Carbohydrate (g):	8
(Calories from fat in beef: 77)		Cholesterol (mg):	71
Fat (g):	9	Sodium (mg):	507

SERVE-A-CROWD BEEF STEAK

Everyone loves a barbecued beef sandwich, and this oven version is great year round. Spoon into crusty rolls or serve in warm flour tortillas with taco-style toppings.

Total preparation and cooking time: 2 hours

3–pound boneless beef round steak, cut 1 inch thick
2 tablespoons chili powder
2 tablespoons packed brown sugar
3 cloves garlic, crushed
1 tablespoon hot pepper sauce
2 medium onions, sliced, separated into rings
1 bottle (12 ounces) chili sauce
10 crusty rolls, split **or** 20 flour tortillas (each about 8 inches), warmed
Toppings: thinly sliced lettuce, julienne-cut jicama, chopped onion, chopped cilantro (optional)

1. Heat oven to 325°. Place 28 × 18-inch piece of heavy duty aluminum foil in shallow roasting pan; place beef steak in center of foil. In small bowl, combine chili powder, brown sugar, garlic and pepper sauce, mixing until well blended. Spread on both sides of steak; top with onions and chili sauce. Bring two opposite sides of foil up over steak; seal with double fold. Seal ends of foil to close. Bake in 325° oven 1½ to 1¾ hours or until beef is tender.

2. Remove onions and juices to medium saucepan. Bring to a boil; cook and stir 3 minutes or until slightly reduced. Meanwhile trim fat from steak. Carve steak crosswise into thin slices; arrange on serving platter. Top with onion mixture. Serve beef in rolls or tortillas with choice of toppings, if desired.

Makes 10 servings (serving size: ¹/₁₀ of recipe).

Nutritional Information Per Serving

Calories:	327	Protein (g):	27
Calories from total fat: 66		Carbohydrate (g):	38
(Calories from fat in beef: 50)		Cholesterol (mg):	66
Fat (g):	7	Sodium (mg):	766

PEPPERY TENDERLOIN STEAKS

A spectacular main dish for guests is easy with these recipes in your repertoire. Begin with versatile top loin steaks simply sprinkled with pepper and broiled. Then choose one of the five savory sauces that follow to add a unique, flavorful finishing touch.

Total preparation and cooking time: 20 minutes

    4 to 8 beef tenderloin steaks, cut 1 inch thick
    ½ to 1 teaspoon cracked black pepper
    ¼ to ½ teaspoon salt

1. Press pepper into both sides of each beef steak. Place steaks on rack in broiler pan so surface of meat is 2 to 3 inches from heat. Broil 10 to 15 minutes for rare to medium doneness, turning once. Trim fat from steaks; season with salt.

2. Serve with Spiced Pear Chutney, Peperonata, Fruited Onion Marmalade, Quick Peppercorn Sauce or Curried Orange Sauce (see pages 155 to 159), if desired.

Makes 4 to 8 servings (serving size: 1 steak).

Nutritional Information Per Serving

Calories:	180	Protein (g):	24
Calories from total fat: 77		Carbohydrate (g):	0
(Calories from fat in beef: 77)		Cholesterol (mg):	71
Fat (g):	9	Sodium (mg):	187

Spiced Pear Chutney

The sweet-hot flavor of a homemade chutney starring pears and raisins seasoned with lime and jalapeño pepper will deliciously complement the beef.

Total preparation and cooking time: 45 minutes

  2 large ripe pears, cored, cut into ½-inch pieces
  1 small onion, chopped
  ⅓ cup cider vinegar
  ⅓ cup sugar
  1 jalapeño pepper, seeded, finely chopped
  2 tablespoons raisins **or** currants
  1 tablespoon fresh lime juice
  ¼ teaspoon ground allspice
  ¼ teaspoon dried thyme leaves

1. In saucepan, combine all ingredients. Bring to a boil; reduce heat to low. Simmer, uncovered, 30 minutes, stirring occasionally. Increase heat to medium-high; cook 5 minutes or until thickened. Serve warm or at room temperature with Peppery Tenderloin Steaks.

Makes 1¼ cups (serving size: ¼ cup).

Nutritional Information Per Serving

Calories:	132	Protein (g):	1
Calories from total fat: 0		Carbohydrate (g):	34
		Cholesterol (mg):	0
Fat (g):	0	Sodium (mg):	2

PEPERONATA

Savor the flavors of sunny Italy with this aromatic blend of colorful bell peppers, onions, and garlic slowly cooked until very tender, almost creamy.

Total preparation and cooking time: 1 hour

- 2 tablespoons olive oil
- 2 red bell peppers, cut lengthwise into thin strips
- 2 yellow bell peppers, cut lengthwise into thin strips
- 1 large red onion, thinly sliced
- 2 large cloves garlic, crushed

1. In large skillet, heat oil over medium-high heat until hot. Add bell peppers, onion and garlic; cook and stir 5 minutes or until tender. Reduce heat to medium-low; cover tightly and continue cooking 40 to 45 minutes or until vegetables are very soft and mixture is almost creamy, stirring occasionally. (If mixture becomes too dry, add 1 to 2 tablespoons water.) Serve warm or at room temperature with Peppery Tenderloin Steaks.

Makes about 2 cups (serving size: ¼ cup).

Nutritional Information Per Serving

Calories:	50	Protein (g):	1
Calories from total fat: 31		Carbohydrate (g):	5
		Cholesterol (mg):	0
Fat (g):	3	Sodium (mg):	2

FRUITED ONION MARMALADE

This piquant mixture of onions cooked until slightly caramelized, dried fruit and cider vinegar is most flavorful served warm with the peppery steaks.

Total preparation and cooking time: 45 minutes

- 1 tablespoon vegetable oil
- 2 medium onions, sliced
- 1 package (8 ounces) mixed dried fruits, coarsely chopped
- 1 cup ready-to-serve beef broth
- 1 tablespoon packed light brown sugar
- 1½ teaspoons cider vinegar
- ¼ teaspoon ground ginger

1. In large nonstick skillet, heat oil over medium-low heat until hot. Add onions; cook slowly 20 minutes or until soft, stirring occasionally.

2. Stir in remaining ingredients. Reduce heat to low; cover tightly and simmer 20 minutes or until fruit is soft, stirring occasionally. Serve warm with Peppery Tenderloin Steaks.

Makes about 2 cups (serving size: ¼ cup).

Nutritional Information Per Serving

Calories:	103	Protein (g):	1
Calories from total fat: 18		Carbohydrate (g):	22
		Cholesterol (mg):	0
Fat (g):	2	Sodium (mg):	104

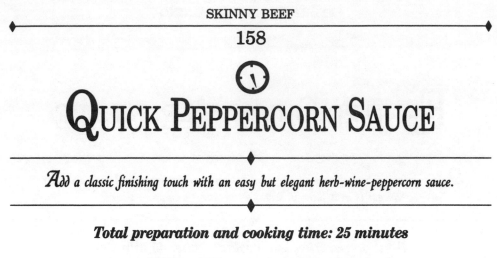

Quick Peppercorn Sauce

Add a classic finishing touch with an easy but elegant herb-wine-peppercorn sauce.

Total preparation and cooking time: 25 minutes

- 1 can (13¾ to 14½ ounces) ready-to-serve beef broth
- 1 tablespoon cornstarch, dissolved in 1 tablespoon water
- 1 small bay leaf
- ⅛ teaspoon dried thyme leaves
- ⅓ cup dry red wine
- ¼ teaspoon black peppercorns, coarsely crushed

1. In saucepan, combine broth and cornstarch mixture, stirring to blend. Bring to a boil; cook until slightly thickened. Stir in bay leaf and thyme; cook over medium-high heat 10 to 12 minutes or until sauce is reduced to about 1 cup.

2. Reduce heat to low. Stir in wine and peppercorns; simmer 5 minutes. Remove bay leaf. Serve warm with Peppery Tenderloin Steaks.

Makes about 1¼ cups (serving size: 1 tablespoon).

Nutritional Information Per Serving

Calories:	6	Protein (g):	0
Calories from total fat: 0		Carbohydrate (g):	0
		Cholesterol (mg):	0
Fat (g):	0	Sodium (mg):	79

CURRIED ORANGE SAUCE

A sauce of orange juice laced with curry, ginger and red pepper lends Indian overtones to beef steaks.

Total preparation and cooking time: 20 minutes

1 tablespoon butter **or** margarine
1 teaspoon curry powder
1 teaspoon grated fresh ginger
1 teaspoon sugar
1 clove garlic, crushed
⅛ teaspoon salt
Dash ground red pepper
1 cup fresh orange juice
1 teaspoon cornstarch, dissolved in 2 teaspoons fresh lemon juice

1. In saucepan, heat butter over low heat until melted. Add curry powder, ginger, sugar, garlic, salt and red pepper; cook and stir 2 to 3 minutes. Increase heat to medium-high. Stir in orange juice; cook until sauce is reduced to ⅔ cup. Add cornstarch mixture; cook and stir 1 minute or until thickened and bubbly. Serve warm with Peppery Tenderloin Steaks.

Makes about ⅔ cup (serving size: 1 tablespoon).

Nutritional Information Per Serving

Calories:	25	Protein (g):	0
Calories from total fat: 11		Carbohydrate (g):	4
		Cholesterol (mg):	3
Fat (g):	1	Sodium (mg):	39

GRILLED ITALIAN STEAK & PASTA

Traditional pasta and sauce gets a makeover when grilled beef steaks accompany the pasta. Fresh tomatoes, basil and Romano cheese flavor this zesty red sauce.

Total preparation and cooking time: 40 minutes

- 3 boneless beef top loin steaks **or** 6 tenderloin steaks, cut 1 inch thick
- 1 tablespoon olive oil
- ¾ cup chopped onion
- 2 large cloves garlic, crushed
- 4 cups chopped plum tomatoes (approx. 1¾ pounds)
- ¾ teaspoon sugar
- ⅛ teaspoon ground nutmeg
- ½ teaspoon salt
- ¼ teaspoon pepper
- 3 tablespoons chopped fresh basil **or** 1 teaspoon dried basil leaves
- 3 tablespoons grated Romano **or** Parmesan cheese
- 2½ cups uncooked penne **or** mostacciollini pasta
  Salt and pepper

1. In large saucepan, heat oil over medium heat until hot. Add onion and garlic; cook and stir until tender. Add tomatoes, sugar, nutmeg, ½ teaspoon salt and ¼ teaspoon pepper; simmer 10 minutes, stirring occasionally. Stir in basil and cheese; cover and remove from heat.

2. Meanwhile cook pasta according to package directions. Keep warm.

3. Place beef steaks on grid over medium coals. Grill steaks 9 to 12 minutes (11 to 13 minutes for tenderloin) for rare to medium doneness, turning once. Season with salt and pepper as desired. Trim fat from steaks. Cut top loin steaks crosswise in half.

4. To serve, spoon tomato sauce over pasta; toss to coat. Serve steaks with pasta.

Cook's Tip: To broil, place steaks on rack in broiler pan so surface of meat is 3 to 4 inches (2 to 3 inches for tenderloin) from heat. Broil steaks 12 to 17 minutes (10 to 15 minutes for tenderloin) for rare to medium doneness, turning once.

Makes 6 servings (serving size: ⅙ of recipe).

Nutritional Information Per Serving

Calories:	391	Protein (g):	32
Calories from total fat: 110		Carbohydrate (g):	38
(Calories from fat in beef: 72)		Cholesterol (mg):	68
Fat (g):	12	Sodium (mg):	466

Beef Sirloin
with Oven-Roasted Vegetables

♦

Potatoes and a colorful assortment of vegetables roast alongside thick-cut sirloin. To complete the menu, add a salad of romaine and sliced oranges drizzled with balsamic vinegar and orange juice.

♦

Total preparation and cooking time: 1¼ hours

- 3–pound boneless beef top sirloin steak, cut 2 inches thick
- 3 cloves garlic, crushed
- 1½ teaspoons dried rosemary leaves, crushed
- ¾ teaspoon salt
- ½ teaspoon pepper
- 2 tablespoons olive oil
- 2 pounds new red potatoes
  Vegetable cooking spray
- 3 medium red, yellow **or** green bell peppers, each cut into 8 wedges
- 3 medium onions, cut into 1-inch thick wedges

1. Heat oven to 425°. Combine garlic, rosemary, salt and pepper; press half of mixture into both sides of beef steak. Add oil to remaining mixture; set aside.

2. Cut small potatoes in half; cut larger ones in quarters. In large bowl, add potatoes and ½ of oil mixture; toss to coat. Lightly spray a 15 × 10-inch jelly roll pan with cooking spray. Arrange potatoes in single layer in pan.

3. In same bowl, combine remaining vegetables and oil mixture; toss to coat. Place beef steak on rack in shallow roasting pan. Insert meat thermometer so bulb is centered in thickest part, not resting in fat. Do not add water. Do not cover. Arrange bell peppers and onions on rack around steak. Place potatoes in oven at the same time.

4. Roast steak and vegetables in 425° oven 45 to 50 minutes until steak is rare to medium doneness and vegetables are tender. Stir potatoes halfway through cooking time. Remove steak when meat thermometer registers 135° for rare, 155° for medium. Let steak stand 10 minutes. (Thick-cut steaks will continue to rise about 5° in temperature to 140° for rare, 160° for medium.)

5. Trim fat from steak. Carve steak crosswise into slices. Serve with vegetables.

Makes 12 servings (serving size: ¹⁄₁₂ of recipe).

Nutritional Information Per Serving

Calories:	261	Protein (g):	28
Calories from total fat: 77		Carbohydrate (g):	17
(Calories from fat in beef: 55)		Cholesterol (mg):	76
Fat (g):	9	Sodium (mg):	196

POACHED BEEF & CARROTS WITH SAVORY SHIITAKE SAUCE

Poaching beef and vegetables is an easy way to make a meal-in-one. Brown the roast (tenderloin or eye round work well) first, then cover with a seasoned liquid such as beef broth and simmer to rare doneness. Baby carrots cook in the liquid with the roast; part of the savory cooking liquid is used to make a sauce.

Total preparation and cooking time: 1 hour

2–pound beef tenderloin **or** eye round roast
1 tablespoon vegetable oil
Water
1 can (10½ ounces) beef consommé
1½ pounds baby carrots
4 large cloves garlic, crushed
4 whole black peppercorns
3 whole cloves
½ ounce dried shiitake mushrooms
2 tablespoons packed brown sugar
2 tablespoons frozen orange juice concentrate, defrosted
2 tablespoons butter **or** margarine
1 teaspoon chopped fresh dill (optional)
2 tablespoons cornstarch, dissolved in 3 tablespoons water
Salt and pepper (optional)

1. In Dutch oven, heat oil over medium heat until hot. Add beef roast; brown evenly. Pour off drippings. Add 4 cups water, consommé, carrots, garlic, peppercorns and cloves. Bring to a boil; reduce heat to medium-low. Cover tightly and simmer 20 minutes (30 minutes for eye round roast) for rare doneness. (Do not overcook.)

2. Remove roast to serving platter. Cover tightly with plastic wrap or aluminum foil and let stand 10 minutes before carving. Reserve 1¾ cups cooking liquid. (Remaining liquid can be used for soup base.)

3. Meanwhile pour ½ cup hot water over mushrooms. Let soak 20 minutes or until mushrooms are softened. Drain well. Remove stems; cut mushrooms into thin strips.

4. In large skillet, heat brown sugar, orange juice concentrate and butter over medium heat until hot and bubbly. Using slotted spoon, remove carrots and add to skillet; cook 5 minutes until glazed. Sprinkle with dill, if desired.

5. Return 1¾ cups cooking liquid to pan; stir in cornstarch mixture. Bring to a boil; cook and stir until thickened. Stir in mushrooms. Season with salt and pepper, if desired.

6. Carve roast into thin slices; serve with sauce and carrots.

Cook's Tip: One-third cup sliced fresh mushrooms may be substituted for dried mushrooms. Do not soak. Lightly sauté before adding to sauce.

Makes 8 servings (serving size: ⅛ of recipe).

Nutritional Information Per Serving

Calories:	313	Protein (g):	28
Calories from total fat: 131		Carbohydrate (g):	17
(Calories from fat in beef: 88)		Cholesterol (mg):	78
Fat (g):	15	Sodium (mg):	496

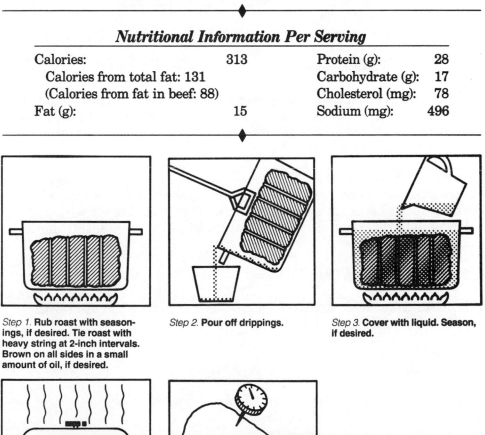

Step 1. **Rub roast with seasonings, if desired. Tie roast with heavy string at 2-inch intervals. Brown on all sides in a small amount of oil, if desired.**

Step 2. **Pour off drippings.**

Step 3. **Cover with liquid. Season, if desired.**

Step 4. **Bring to a boil. Reduce heat; cover and gently simmer.**

Step 5. **Cover tightly with plastic wrap or aluminum foil and let stand 10 minutes before carving.**

CHILI-ROASTED SIRLOIN WITH CORN PUDDING

Use Spicy Seasoning Mix to add flavor and flair to roasted thick-cut sirloin. A super easy version of Corn Pudding made with a corn muffin mix bakes alongside the steak.

Total preparation and cooking time: 1¼ hours

> 3–pound boneless beef top sirloin steak, cut
>   2 inches thick
> 1 tablespoon Spicy Seasoning Mix (see page 39)
> 2 large cloves garlic, crushed
>   Salt and pepper

1. Heat oven to 350°. Combine seasoning mix and garlic; press into both sides of beef steak. Place steak on rack in shallow roasting pan. Insert meat thermometer so bulb is centered in thickest part, not resting in fat. Do not add water. Do not cover.

2. Roast in 350° oven 50 to 60 minutes for rare to medium doneness. Remove steak when meat thermometer registers 135° for rare, 155° for medium. Let steak stand 10 minutes. (Thick-cut steaks will continue to rise about 5° in temperature to 140° for rare, 160° for medium.)

3. Meanwhile prepare Corn Pudding.

4. Trim fat from steak. Carve steak crosswise into slices. Season with salt and pepper, as desired. Serve with Corn Pudding.

Corn Pudding

> 1 bag (20 ounces) frozen corn, defrosted
> 2 small onions, quartered
> 2 cups low-fat milk
> 2 eggs, beaten
> 1 package (8½ ounces) corn muffin mix
> ½ teaspoon salt
> ½ cup shredded Cheddar cheese
> 1 cup thinly sliced romaine lettuce
> ½ cup julienne-cut radishes

1. Heat oven to 350°. In food processor, fitted with steel blade, combine corn and onions. Cover; process, pulsing on and off, until corn is broken but not pureed, scraping side of bowl as necessary. Add milk and eggs; pulse just until blended. Add muffin mix and salt; pulse just until blended.

2. Pour mixture into greased 11 × 7-inch baking dish. Bake in 350° oven 45 minutes or until lightly browned.

3. Sprinkle cheese over pudding; place under broiler so surface is 3 to 4 inches from heat. Broil 4 minutes or until cheese is melted and top is crusty. To serve, garnish with lettuce and radishes.

Makes 12 servings (serving size: ¹⁄₁₂ of recipes).

Nutritional Information Per Serving

Calories:	353	Protein (g):	33
Calories from total fat: 112		Carbohydrate (g):	28
(Calories from fat in beef: 55)		Cholesterol (mg):	129
Fat (g):	13	Sodium (mg):	564

CHEESY SPINACH STUFFED MEATLOAF

♦

Think of this festive main dish as a gourmet meatloaf. A zesty and colorful spinach and cheese filling is rolled up inside the ground beef. Thick potato wedges seasoned with herbs can bake alongside. (See photograph)

♦

Total preparation and cooking time: 1½ hours

Meatloaf
- 1½ pounds lean ground beef
- ¾ cup soft bread crumbs
- 1 egg
- 1 teaspoon salt
- ⅛ teaspoon pepper

Filling
- 1 package (10 ounces) frozen chopped spinach, defrosted, well drained
- ½ cup shredded part-skim mozzarella cheese
- 3 tablespoons grated Parmesan cheese
- 1 teaspoon Italian seasoning
- ¼ teaspoon salt (optional)
- ⅛ teaspoon garlic powder

Topping
- 3 tablespoons ketchup
- ¼ cup shredded part-skim mozzarella cheese
- Italian seasoning (optional)

1. Heat oven to 350°. In large bowl, combine meatloaf ingredients, mixing lightly but thoroughly. In medium bowl, combine filling ingredients; mix well. Set aside.

2. Place beef mixture on waxed paper and pat into 14 × 10-inch rectangle. Spread filling over beef, leaving ¾-inch border around edges. Starting at short end, roll up jelly-roll fashion. Press beef mixture over spinach filling at both ends to seal. Place seam side down on rack in open roasting pan.

3. Bake in 350° oven 1 hour. Spread ketchup over loaf; return to oven and continue baking 15 minutes. Top loaf with ¼ cup mozzarella cheese. Sprinkle with additional Italian seasoning, if desired.

4. To serve, cut into 1-inch thick slices.

Cook's Tip: To make soft bread crumbs, place torn bread slices in food processor, fitted with steel blade, or blender container. Cover; process 30 seconds, pulsing on and off, until fine crumbs. One and a half slices will yield 1 cup soft bread crumbs.

Makes 6 servings (serving size: two 1-inch thick slices).

Nutritional Information Per Serving

Calories:	272	Protein (g):	30
Calories from total fat: 123		Carbohydrate (g):	8
(Calories from fat in beef: 82)		Cholesterol (mg):	115
Fat (g):	14	Sodium (mg):	729

BEEF KABOBS *AU POIVRE* WITH BROCCOLI PILAF

Kabobs always impress and, with the colorful pilaf, this complete main dish can be on the table in 30 minutes. If you use bamboo skewers, be sure to soak skewers in water before using.

Total preparation and cooking time: 30 minutes

    1- pound boneless beef top sirloin steak, cut
        1¼ inches thick
    2 teaspoons vegetable oil
    2 teaspoons coarse-grain Dijon-style mustard
    2 teaspoons red wine vinegar
    1 clove garlic, crushed
    ½ teaspoon cracked black pepper

1. Prepare Broccoli Pilaf.

2. Meanwhile trim fat from beef steak. Cut steak into 1-inch pieces. In medium bowl, combine oil, mustard, vinegar, garlic and pepper; add beef, tossing to coat.

3. Thread equal amount of beef onto each of four 12-inch metal skewers. Place kabobs on rack in broiler pan so surface of meat is 3 to 4 inches from heat. Broil 9 to 12 minutes for rare to medium doneness, turning occasionally. Serve with Broccoli Pilaf.

Broccoli Pilaf

    1 small onion, chopped
    1 clove garlic, crushed
    2 teaspoons vegetable oil
    ⅔ cup uncooked regular long grain rice
    1¼ cups ready-to-serve beef broth
    1 tablespoon coarse-grain Dijon-style mustard
    4 cups small broccoli florets

1. In large saucepan, cook and stir onion and garlic in oil over medium heat until tender. Add rice and cook 1 minute more. Stir in broth and mustard. Bring to a boil; reduce heat to low. Cover and simmer 15 minutes. Place broccoli over rice; cover and continue cooking 7 minutes or until broccoli and rice are tender. Stir before serving. Serve immediately.

Makes 4 servings (serving size: 1 kabob and 1 cup pilaf).

Nutritional Information Per Serving

Calories:	382	Protein (g):	33
Calories from total fat: 105		Carbohydrate (g):	36
(Calories from fat in beef: 55)		Cholesterol (mg):	76
Fat (g):	12	Sodium (mg):	404

PEPPERED BEEF & PEAR SALAD

This sophisticated main dish salad pairs warm slices of roasted beef tenderloin with cool, crisp salad greens and buttery pear slices. Honey and rice wine vinegar give the ginger dressing a sweet-sour tang.

Total preparation and cooking time: 1 hour
Marinating time: 30 minutes

2–pound beef tenderloin roast
2 teaspoons cracked black pepper
  Mixed salad greens
2 firm ripe red Bartlett pears, cored, each
  cut lengthwise into 8 wedges
2 firm ripe yellow Bartlett pears, cored, each
  cut lengthwise into 8 wedges
  Chives and raspberries (optional)

Marinade
¼ cup soy sauce
¼ cup dry white wine
3 tablespoons honey
2 teaspoons dark sesame oil

Honey-Ginger Dressing
⅓ cup rice wine vinegar
2 tablespoons vegetable oil
2 tablespoons water
1 tablespoon snipped chives
1½ teaspoons grated fresh ginger
1½ teaspoons honey
¼ teaspoon salt

1. Combine marinade ingredients, stirring well. Place beef roast in plastic bag; add marinade, turning to coat. Close bag securely and marinate in refrigerator 30 minutes, turning once. Remove roast from marinade; pat dry. Discard marinade.

2. Heat oven to 425°. Press pepper evenly into surface of roast. Place roast on rack in shallow roasting pan. Insert meat thermometer so bulb is centered in thickest part, not resting in fat. Do not add water. Do not cover.

3. Roast in 425° oven 35 to 45 minutes for rare to medium doneness. Remove roast when meat thermometer registers 135° for rare, 155°for medium. Let stand 10 minutes. (Roasts will continue to rise

about 5° in temperature to 140° for rare, 160° for medium.) Trim fat from roast. Carve roast into ¼-inch thick slices.

4. Meanwhile in small bowl, whisk together dressing ingredients.

5. To serve, place salad greens on 8 individual plates. Alternately arrange 3 beef slices and 2 red and 2 yellow pear wedges in a fan on salad greens. Garnish with chives and raspberries, if desired. Serve with dressing.

Makes 8 servings (serving size: ⅛ of recipe).

Nutritional Information Per Serving

Calories:	307	Protein (g):	26
Calories from total fat: 128		Carbohydrate (g):	20
(Calories from fat in beef: 88)		Cholesterol (mg):	71
Fat (g):	14	Sodium (mg):	403

- Place roast (straight from refrigerator), fat side up, on rack in a shallow roasting pan.
- Insert a meat thermometer into thickest part of roast, not touching bone or fat.
- Do not add water. Do not cover.
- Roast to 5 to 10 degrees below desired doneness.

- Allow roast to stand 15 to 20 minutes before serving, as it will also be easier to carve.
- Carve cooked roast across the grain into thin slices.

SAVORY BEEF STEW WITH ROASTED VEGETABLES

◆

Vegetables roasted with a drizzling of balsamic vinegar take on a slightly caramelized flavor—a tasty complement to the beef, which simmers to fork tenderness in a garlic and thyme flavored broth. Quick-cooking couscous makes a good accompaniment.
(See photograph)

◆

Total preparation and cooking time: 2½ hours

1¾ to 2   pounds boneless beef chuck shoulder **or** bottom round
    1   tablespoon olive oil
    3   cloves garlic, crushed
    ¾   teaspoon pepper
    1   can (13¾ to 14½ ounces) ready-to-serve beef broth
    2   teaspoons dried thyme leaves
       Vegetable cooking spray
  12   medium mushrooms
    6   plum tomatoes, each cut lengthwise into quarters, seeded
    3   small onions, each cut lengthwise into quarters
  1½   tablespoons olive oil
  1½   tablespoons plus 2 teaspoons balsamic vinegar (divided)
    1   tablespoon cornstarch, dissolved in 2 tablespoons water
       Chopped fresh thyme (optional)
    3   cups cooked couscous

1. Trim fat from beef. Cut beef into 1-inch pieces. In Dutch oven, heat 1 tablespoon oil over medium heat until hot. Add beef and garlic (half at a time) and brown evenly, stirring occasionally. Pour off drippings. Season with pepper. Stir in broth and dried thyme. Bring to a boil; reduce heat to low. Cover tightly and simmer 1½ to 2 hours or until beef is tender.

2. Meanwhile heat oven to 425°. Lightly spray 15 × 10-inch jelly roll pan with cooking spray. Place vegetables in pan. Combine 1½ tablespoons oil and 1½ tablespoons vinegar; drizzle over vegetables, tossing to coat. Roast in 425° oven 20 to 25 minutes or until tender.

3. Bring beef stew to a boil over medium-high heat. Add cornstarch mixture; cook and stir 2 minutes or until sauce is slightly thickened and bubbly. Stir in roasted vegetables and remaining 2 teaspoons vinegar. Sprinkle with fresh thyme, if desired. Serve with couscous.

Makes 6 servings (serving size: ⅙ of recipe).

Nutritional Information Per Serving

Calories:	380	Protein (g):	34
Calories from total fat: 121		Carbohydrate (g):	30
(Calories from fat in beef: 63)		Cholesterol (mg):	86
Fat (g):	13	Sodium (mg):	281

Chunky Beef Chili

A buffet-style chili party can be a nearly effortless way to entertain when most of the work is done ahead of time. Make the chili the day before and refrigerate. While the chili reheats, assemble the toppings.

Total preparation and cooking time: 2 hours

2½ pounds boneless beef chuck arm pot roast
2   tablespoons vegetable oil
1   cup coarsely chopped onion
1   cup chopped green bell pepper
2   cloves garlic, crushed
1   teaspoon salt
2   cans (14½ to 16 ounces) Mexican-style diced tomatoes, undrained
1   can (6 ounces) tomato paste
3   tablespoons chili powder
1   teaspoon dried oregano leaves
¼ to ½ teaspoon crushed red pepper
    Toppings: sliced green onions, drained and rinsed black beans, dairy sour cream, sliced jalapeño pepper (optional)

1. Trim fat from beef. Cut beef into ½-inch pieces. In Dutch oven, heat oil over medium heat until hot. Add beef, onion, bell pepper and garlic (half at a time) and brown beef evenly, stirring occasionally. Pour off drippings.

2. Season beef with salt. Stir in tomatoes, tomato paste, chili powder, oregano and red pepper. Bring to a boil; reduce heat to low. Cover tightly and simmer 1½ hours or until beef is tender.

3. Serve with choice of toppings, if desired.

Makes 8 servings (serving size: 1 cup).

Nutritional Information Per Serving

Calories:	280	Protein (g):	31
Calories from total fat: 103		Carbohydrate (g):	15
(Calories from fat in beef: 63)		Cholesterol (mg):	86
Fat (g):	11	Sodium (mg):	705

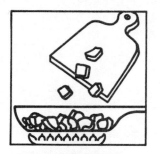

Step 1. **Coat meat with seasoned flour, if desired. Brown on all sides in small amount of oil, if desired.**

Step 2. **Pour off drippings.**

Step 3. **Cover with liquid. Season, if desired.**

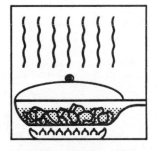

Step 4. **Cover tightly and simmer on stove top or in oven until meat is tender. Add vegetables, if desired, toward end of cooking time.**

10.
CLASSIC FAVORITES 90s' STYLE

$\boxed{\text{S}}$ ome beef dishes never go out of style. Meatloaf, lasagna and Swiss steak, for example. As popular as they may be, these classics can still benefit from a little updating to make them easier, quicker, more healthful and ultimately more flavorful.

In this chapter, fresh vegetable and beef soup is on the table in 30 minutes. Beef Wellington 90s' style is minus the paté and puffed pastry but has all the flavor you'd expect. Country-fried steak is lean and quick.

These delicious updates are accomplished in a variety of ways that are easy to do at home:

- Use timesaving appliances such as the microwave oven and food processor.
- Cook with high quality convenience products in combination with fresh.
- Substitute lower-fat ingredients whenever possible.
- Use smart cooking techniques that require little or no added fat.

QUICK STEAK & VEGETABLE SOUP

A homemade soup nourishes and comforts on a cold night. This one is made with bite-sized pieces of beef and veggies that cook to fork tenderness in minutes—not hours. (See photograph)

Total preparation and cooking time: 30 minutes

- 1–pound boneless beef top sirloin steak, cut ¾ inch thick
- 2 cans (13¾ to 14½ ounces each) ready-to-serve beef broth
- 1 large onion, chopped
- ½ pound all-purpose potatoes, cut into ½-inch pieces
- ½ pound baby carrots
- 1 cup frozen peas
- ¼ cup chopped assorted fresh herbs (parsley, chives, thyme, basil)
- 2 tablespoons balsamic **or** red wine vinegar
- 2 teaspoons vegetable oil
- ½ teaspoon coarse grind black pepper

1. Trim fat from beef steak. Cut steak lengthwise into three strips and then crosswise into ½-inch thick pieces.

2. In large saucepan, combine broth, onion, potatoes, carrots and peas. Bring to a boil; reduce heat to low. Simmer, uncovered, 15 minutes or until vegetables are tender. Stir in herbs and vinegar.

3. Meanwhile in large nonstick skillet, heat oil over medium-high heat until hot. Add beef (half at a time) and stir-fry 2 to 3 minutes or until outside surface is no longer pink. (Do not overcook.) Season with pepper. Place equal amount of beef into 4 individual soup bowls.

4. To serve, ladle vegetables and broth mixture over beef. Serve immediately.

Makes 4 servings (serving size: 1¾ cups).

Nutritional Information Per Serving

Calories:	316	Protein (g):	32
Calories from total fat: 83		Carbohydrate (g):	26
(Calories from fat in beef: 55)		Cholesterol (mg):	76
Fat (g):	9	Sodium (mg):	758

COUNTRY-FRIED STEAK

In 20 minutes, country-fried steak as good as Mom's! It's crisp, spicy on the outside and tender, juicy inside.

Total preparation and cooking time: 20 minutes

- 4 beef bottom round cubed steaks (approx. 4 ounces each)
- 2 egg whites
- 2 tablespoons low-fat milk
- 2 tablespoons vegetable oil

Coating
- ½ cup dry bread crumbs
- 1 tablespoon cornmeal
- ½ teaspoon Spicy Seasoning Mix (see page 39)
- ¼ teaspoon salt
- ¼ teaspoon pepper

Toppings
- ½ cup prepared salsa
- ½ cup nonfat plain yogurt

1. In medium bowl, beat egg whites and milk until blended. In shallow dish, combine coating ingredients. Dip each beef steak into egg white mixture, then coating mixture to coat both sides.

2. In large nonstick skillet, heat oil over medium to medium-high heat until hot. Place steaks in skillet; cook 5 to 6 minutes, turning once.

3. To serve, pass salsa and yogurt.

Makes 4 servings (serving size: ¼ of recipe).

Nutritional Information Per Serving

Calories:	334	Protein (g):	32
Calories from total fat: 131		Carbohydrate (g):	16
(Calories from fat in beef: 63)		Cholesterol (mg):	83
Fat (g):	15	Sodium (mg):	549

UPDATED BEEF STROGANOFF

Updated Beef Stroganoff goes from skillet to dinner plate in minutes. By passing the sour half-and-half instead of adding it to the sauce, you can use less. (See photograph)

Total preparation and cooking time: 25 minutes

  1   pound beef tenderloin tips
1½   cups uncooked farfalle (bow tie) pasta
        Vegetable cooking spray
  ¼   teaspoon salt
  ⅛   teaspoon pepper
  ½   pound mushrooms, cut into ½-inch slices
  ⅓   cup coarsely chopped onion
  2   teaspoons vegetable oil
1 to 2 tablespoons all-purpose flour
  ¾   cup ready-to-serve beef broth
  1   tablespoon sliced green onion
  ¼   cup dairy sour half-and-half

1. Cook pasta according to package directions. Keep warm.

2. Meanwhile trim fat from beef; cut into 1×½-inch pieces. Spray large nonstick skillet with cooking spray. Heat skillet over medium-high heat until hot. Add beef (half at a time) and stir-fry 1 to 2 minutes or until outside surface is no longer pink. Remove from skillet; keep warm. Season with salt and pepper.

3. In same skillet, cook mushrooms and onion in oil 2 minutes or until tender; stir in flour. Gradually add broth, stirring until blended. Bring to a boil; cook and stir 2 minutes. Return beef to skillet; heat through.

4. Serve beef mixture over pasta. Sprinkle with green onion; pass sour half-and-half to dollop on top.

Cook's Tip: One-pound boneless beef top sirloin steak, cut ¾ inch thick, may be substituted for beef tenderloin tips. Cut steak lengthwise in half and then crosswise into ¼-inch thick strips.

Makes 4 servings (serving size: ¼ of recipe).

Nutritional Information Per Serving

Calories:	344	Protein (g):	30
Calories from total fat: 121		Carbohydrate (g):	25
(Calories from fat in beef: 77)		Cholesterol (mg):	77
Fat (g):	13	Sodium (mg):	344

Swiss Steak Piperade

Cooking less tender cuts of beef to fork tenderness is simple to do. The beef should be simmered, not boiled, to ensure tenderness. Adding color and garden-fresh flavor to this updated classic is a piperade (pee-pay-RAHD)—a blend of tomatoes and sweet bell peppers. Serve over rice or pasta.

Total preparation and cooking time: 2 hours

1¾ pounds boneless beef chuck shoulder steaks **or** round steak, cut ¾ inch thick
1 tablespoon vegetable oil
¾ teaspoon salt
½ teaspoon dried thyme leaves
¼ teaspoon pepper
1 large onion, chopped
1 to 2 medium jalapeño peppers, cut into ⅛-inch slices
¼ cup water
4 medium tomatoes, chopped
½ green bell pepper, cut into 1-inch pieces
½ yellow bell pepper, cut into 1-inch pieces
3 cups cooked rice **or** pasta
1 tablespoon chopped fresh parsley

1. Heat oven to 325°. In large ovenproof skillet or Dutch oven, heat oil over medium-high heat until hot. Place beef steaks in skillet and brown on both sides. Pour off drippings, if necessary. Season steaks with salt, thyme and pepper; top with onion and jalapeño pepper. Add water. Cover tightly and simmer in 325° oven 45 minutes.

2. Add tomatoes and bell peppers. Cover and continue cooking 30 minutes or until beef and vegetables are tender. Remove beef to warm platter.

3. On stove top, continue to cook over high heat 8 to 10 minutes or until sauce is reduced and slightly thickened, stirring frequently.

4. Trim fat from steaks. Cut steaks into serving size pieces; return to sauce mixture. Serve over rice; garnish with parsley.

Cook's Tip: Remove interior ribs and seeds from jalapeño peppers if a milder flavor is desired.

Makes 6 servings (serving size: ⅙ of recipe).

Nutritional Information Per Serving

Calories:	373	Protein (g):	32
Calories from total fat: 90		Carbohydrate (g):	37
(Calories from fat in beef: 63)		Cholesterol (mg):	86
Fat (g):	10	Sodium (mg):	333

No-Fuss Beef & Spinach Lasagna

There's no need to precook the noodles for this no-fuss lasagna—the noodles cook during baking.

Total preparation and cooking time: 65 minutes

1	pound lean ground beef
¼	teaspoon salt
1	jar **or** can (26 to 30 ounces) prepared low-fat spaghetti sauce
1	can (14½ ounces) Italian-style diced tomatoes, undrained
¼	teaspoon ground red pepper
1	carton (15 ounces) part-skim ricotta cheese
1	package (10 ounces) frozen chopped spinach, defrosted, well drained
¼	cup grated Parmesan cheese
1	egg, beaten
10	uncooked lasagna noodles
1½	cups shredded part-skim mozzarella cheese

1. Heat oven to 375°. In large nonstick skillet, brown ground beef over medium heat 8 to 10 minutes or until no longer pink. Pour off drippings. Season with salt; add spaghetti sauce, tomatoes and red pepper, stirring to combine. Set aside.

2. Meanwhile in medium bowl, combine ricotta cheese, spinach, Parmesan cheese and egg. Spread 2 cups beef sauce over bottom of 13 × 9-inch baking dish. Arrange 4 lasagna noodles lengthwise in single layer. Place 5th noodle across end of baking dish, breaking noodle to fit dish; press noodles into sauce. Spread entire ricotta cheese mixture on top of noodles; sprinkle with 1 cup mozzarella cheese and top with 1½ cups beef sauce. Arrange remaining noodles in single layer; press lightly into sauce. Top with remaining beef sauce.

3. Bake in 375° oven 45 minutes or until noodles are tender. Sprinkle remaining mozzarella cheese on top; tent lightly with aluminum foil. Let stand 15 minutes before cutting into 12 squares.

Makes 12 servings (serving size: one 3 x 3-inch square).

Nutritional Information Per Serving

Calories:	261	Protein (g):	21
Calories from total fat: 87		Carbohydrate (g):	23
(Calories from fat in beef: 27)		Cholesterol (mg):	61
Fat (g):	10	Sodium (mg):	555

Mini Beef Wellingtons

Gone are the overly rich paté and puffed pastry, replaced by paper-thin sheets of phyllo and a seasoned mushroom filling. This updated classic, special enough for the most elegant at-home entertaining, can be prepared and served in under an hour! (See photograph)

Total preparation and cooking time: 40 minutes

4 small beef tenderloin steaks, cut 1 inch thick
  (3 to 4 ounces each)
2 teaspoons olive oil
½ pound mushrooms, finely chopped
3 tablespoons dry red wine
3 tablespoons finely chopped green onions
¼ teaspoon dried thyme leaves
  Salt and pepper
6 phyllo dough sheets, defrosted
  Vegetable cooking spray

1. Heat oven to 425°. In large nonstick skillet, heat oil over medium-high heat until hot. Add mushrooms; cook and stir until tender. Add wine; cook 2 to 3 minutes or until liquid is evaporated. Stir in green onions, thyme, ¼ teaspoon salt and ⅛ teaspoon pepper. Remove from skillet; cool thoroughly.

2. Heat same skillet over medium-high heat until hot. Place steaks in skillet; cook 3 minutes, turning once. (Steaks will be partially cooked. Do not overcook.) Season with salt and pepper, as desired.

3. On flat surface, layer phyllo dough, spraying each sheet thoroughly with cooking spray. Cut stacked layers lengthwise in half and then crosswise to make 4 equal portions. Place about 2 tablespoons mushroom mixture in center of each portion; spread mixture to diameter of each steak. Place steaks on mushroom mixture. Bring together all 4 corners of phyllo dough; twist tightly to close. Lightly spray each with cooking spray; place on greased baking sheet.

4. Immediately bake in 425° oven 9 to 10 minutes or until golden brown. Let stand 5 minutes. Serve immediately.

Makes 4 servings (serving size: ¼ of recipe).

Nutritional Information Per Serving

Calories:	277	Protein (g):	26
Calories from total fat: 119		Carbohydrate (g):	11
(Calories from fat in beef: 88)		Cholesterol (mg):	71
Fat (g):	13	Sodium (mg):	232

EASY STEAK DIANE

One-skillet preparation and a creamy sauce that's four-ingredients-quick make this American classic extra easy. Serve with your favorite pasta and a berry shortcake for dessert.

Total preparation and cooking time: 25 minutes

2 boneless beef top loin steaks, cut 1 inch thick
1 tablespoon vegetable oil
½ pound small mushrooms, cut into ¼-inch slices
2 tablespoons finely chopped shallots **or** green onion
1 teaspoon grated lemon peel
¼ teaspoon pepper
Vegetable cooking spray
1 tablespoon brandy (optional)
1 tablespoon fresh lemon juice
2 teaspoons Worcestershire sauce
2 teaspoons Dijon-style mustard
¼ cup half-and-half
1 pound asparagus, steamed

1. In large nonstick skillet, heat oil over medium heat until hot. Add mushrooms and shallots; cook and stir 3 minutes or until tender. Remove from skillet; wipe out with paper towels.

2. Combine lemon peel and pepper; press into both sides of beef steaks. Spray same skillet with cooking spray. Heat skillet over medium heat until hot. Place steaks in skillet; cook 9 to 11 minutes for rare to medium doneness, turning once. Remove and keep warm.

3. If desired, add brandy to same skillet; cook and stir until browned bits attached to skillet are dissolved. Return mushroom mixture to skillet. Add combined lemon juice, Worcestershire sauce, mustard and half-and-half; cook and stir until heated through.

4. Trim fat from steaks. Carve steaks crosswise into thick slices. Spoon some of sauce over beef. Pass remaining sauce. Serve with asparagus.

Cook's Tip: To steam asparagus spears, place steamer basket in ½ inch water (water should not touch bottom of basket). Place asparagus in basket. Cover tightly and heat to boiling; reduce heat. Steam 6 to 8 minutes or until crisp-tender.

Makes 4 servings (serving size: ¼ of recipe).

Nutritional Information Per Serving

Calories:	275	Protein (g):	29
Calories from total fat: 124		Carbohydrate (g):	10
(Calories from fat in beef: 72)		Cholesterol (mg):	70
Fat (g):	14	Sodium (mg):	128

CLASSIC MEATLOAF

◆

By shaping the ground beef mixture into small, two-serving loaves, baking time can be reduced by 30 minutes. Gentle handling when mixing the ground beef with the other ingredients will ensure a moist, tender meatloaf.

◆

Total preparation and cooking time: 1 hour

1½ pounds lean ground beef
1 can (8 ounces) tomato sauce
1 cup soft bread crumbs
1 small onion, finely chopped
1 egg, slightly beaten
2 teaspoons Worcestershire sauce
1 teaspoon dried thyme leaves
½ teaspoon garlic salt
¼ teaspoon pepper
1 tablespoon packed brown sugar
1 teaspoon dry mustard

1. Heat oven to 350°. Reserve ¼ cup tomato sauce. In large bowl, combine ground beef, remaining tomato sauce, bread crumbs, onion, egg, Worcestershire sauce, thyme, garlic salt and pepper, mixing lightly but thoroughly.

2. Divide mixture into thirds and shape to form three loaves, each about 1½ inches thick; place on rack in open roasting pan. Combine reserved tomato sauce, brown sugar and mustard; spread over top of loaves.

3. Bake in 350° oven 40 to 45 minutes or until no longer pink and juices run clear. To serve, cut each meatloaf into 1-inch thick slices.

Cook's Tip: To make soft bread crumbs, place torn bread slices in food processor, fitted with steel blade, or blender container. Cover; process 30 seconds, pulsing on and off, until fine crumbs. One and a half slices will yield 1 cup soft bread crumbs.

Makes 6 servings (serving size: ½ loaf).

Nutritional Information Per Serving

Calories:	229	Protein (g):	24
Calories from total fat: 93		Carbohydrate (g):	10
(Calories from fat in beef: 82)		Cholesterol (mg):	105
Fat (g):	10	Sodium (mg):	517

BEEF & LENTIL SOUP

Ready-to-use tomatoes, beef broth and lentils are the secret to this quick-fix soup. Because lean beef tip steaks can overcook in a flash, they're added to the soup pot just before serving. Crisp apple wedges, your favorite cheese and French bread are effortless accompaniments.

Total preparation and cooking time: 45 minutes

½ to ¾ pound beef round tip steaks, cut ⅛ to ¼ inch thick
2 teaspoons vegetable oil
1 medium onion, chopped
2 large cloves garlic, crushed
2 cups water
1 can (13¾ to 14½ ounces) ready-to-serve beef broth
1 jar (8 ounces) medium picante sauce **or** salsa
¾ cup dried lentils, rinsed
2 cups thinly sliced escarole **or** spinach leaves

1. In Dutch oven, heat oil over medium heat until hot. Add onion and garlic; cook and stir 3 to 5 minutes or until tender. Add water, broth, picante sauce and lentils. Bring to a boil; reduce heat to low. Cover tightly and simmer 35 to 45 minutes or until lentils are tender.

2. Meanwhile trim fat from beef steaks. Stack steaks and cut lengthwise in half and then crosswise into 1-inch wide strips; set aside.

3. Increase heat to medium; bring to a boil. Stir in beef and escarole. Immediately remove from heat. Cover and let stand 5 minutes before serving.

Makes 4 servings (serving size: 1¾ cups).

Nutritional Information Per Serving

Calories:	290	Protein (g):	28
Calories from total fat: 61		Carbohydrate (g):	28
(Calories from fat in beef: 35)		Cholesterol (mg):	46
Fat (g):	7	Sodium (mg):	751

Easy Beef Stuffed Peppers

The microwave oven precooks the bell peppers for this family favorite in minutes. Italian-style diced tomatoes save time, too—they're seasoned and ready to use.

Total preparation and cooking time: 55 minutes

4 medium green, red **or** yellow bell peppers

Filling
- 1 pound lean ground beef
- ¾ cup chopped onion
- 1 cup cooked rice
- 2 tablespoons ketchup
- ½ teaspoon dried oregano leaves
- ½ teaspoon salt (optional)
- ¼ teaspoon pepper

Topping
- 1 can (14½ ounces) Italian-style diced tomatoes, undrained
- 1 tablespoon ketchup
- ½ teaspoon dried oregano leaves

1. Heat oven to 350°. Cut bell peppers lengthwise in half; remove seeds. Place cut side down in microwave-safe oblong baking dish. Microwave, uncovered, at high 4 minutes. Turn cut side up.

2. In medium bowl, combine filling ingredients, mixing lightly but thoroughly. Spoon about ½ cup beef mixture into each bell pepper half.

3. In small bowl, combine topping ingredients; spoon over bell pepper halves. Cover dish tightly with foil. Bake in 350° oven 40 to 45 minutes or until beef mixture is cooked.

4. To serve, place peppers on serving platter. Spoon pan juices over top.

Makes 4 servings (serving size: 2 stuffed pepper halves).

Nutritional Information Per Serving

Calories:	318	Protein (g):	26
Calories from total fat: 86		Carbohydrate (g):	34
(Calories from fat in beef: 82)		Cholesterol (mg):	70
Fat (g):	10	Sodium (mg):	556

UPDATED BEEF BOURGUIGNONNE

◆

Beef burgundy stew has long been a staple of French family-style cooking. A crusty French bread, crisp salad and apple tart are traditional accompaniments.

◆

Total preparation and cooking time: 2½ hours

2½ pounds boneless beef chuck arm pot roast
¾ teaspoon dried marjoram leaves
¾ teaspoon pepper
  Vegetable cooking spray
1 can (13¾ to 14½ ounces) ready-to-serve beef broth
1 cup Burgundy wine
2 cloves garlic, crushed
1 bag (1 pound) baby carrots
½ pound small mushrooms
1 large onion, cut into 1-inch pieces
2 to 2½ tablespoons cornstarch, dissolved in ¼ cup water

1. Trim fat from beef. Cut beef into 1-inch pieces. Combine marjoram and pepper; sprinkle over beef. Spray Dutch oven with cooking spray; heat over medium heat until hot. Add beef (half at a time) and brown evenly, stirring occasionally. Pour off drippings.

2. Stir in broth, wine and garlic. Bring to a boil; reduce heat to low. Cover tightly and simmer 1½ hours. Add carrots, mushrooms and onion. Cover and continue cooking 30 minutes or until beef and vegetables are tender.

3. Stir in cornstarch mixture. Bring to a boil; cook and stir 1 minute or until thickened.

Cook's Tip: One pound medium carrots, peeled and cut into 1-inch pieces, may be substituted for baby carrots.

Makes 8 servings (serving size: 1 cup).

Nutritional Information Per Serving

Calories:	258	Protein (g):	30
Calories from total fat: 67		Carbohydrate (g):	12
(Calories from fat in beef: 63)		Cholesterol (mg):	86
Fat (g):	7	Sodium (mg):	239

Step 1. **Coat meat with seasoned flour, if desired. Brown on all sides in small amount of oil, if desired.**

Step 2. **Pour off drippings.**

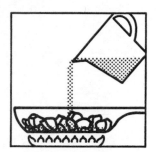

Step 3. **Cover with liquid. Season, if desired.**

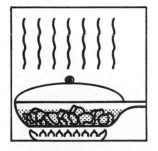

Step 4. **Cover tightly and simmer on stove top or in oven until meat is tender. Add vegetables, if desired, toward end of cooking time.**

GLOSSARY

The following are explanations of ingredients and cooking terms used in the recipes in this book.

Apples (cooking)—Apple varieties that remain flavorful and firm even after cooking include: Baldwin, Cortland, Northern Spy, Rome Beauty, Jonathan, Winesap and Granny Smith.

Artichoke Hearts (marinated)—The tender centers of the artichoke marinated in oil and seasonings.

Au Poivre—A French term meaning peppered.

Balsamic Vinegar—An Italian vinegar dark in color with a unique, pungent sweet flavor. Aged in barrels of various woods over a period of years.

Bourguignonne—Literally translated as "prepared in the style of Burgundy," a famous French cooking region. Refers to meat cooked in red wine, usually garnished with small mushrooms and onions.

Carne Asada—A Spanish term meaning "grilled steak."

Chives—An herb with long, slender, dark green stems and a delicate onion flavor. Chives are related to onions and leeks.

Chutney—A spicy condiment, East Indian in origin, usually made of fruit, vinegar, sugar and spices. Chutneys range from chunky to smooth and mild to hot. Often served as an accompaniment to curried dishes.

Cilantro—Also known as coriander and Chinese parsley, this herb is related to the parsley family. Fresh leaves have a distinctive, earthy flavor often used in cuisines of India, Mexico, the Orient and the Caribbean.

Couscous—A fine, precooked semolina (a pasta base made from durum wheat) that cooks up into small pale yellow nuggets. Often served as a side dish.

Crisp-Tender—A term used to describe vegetables that are cooked just until tender so they are still crisp and brightly colored, not soft.

Curry—A blend of many spices, including ginger, coriander, cumin, turmeric, black pepper and dried red chilies. It gives a yellow color to foods and is often used in Indian cookery.

Deglaze—To make a sauce by adding a small amount of liquid to a pan in which meat has been sautéed, heating it and stirring to loosen browned bits of food on the bottom of the pan.

Dry Rub—A blend of crushed herbs, spices and sometimes salt that is rubbed onto the surface of steaks and roasts prior to cooking to add flavor.

Dutch Oven—A large, deep pot with a tight-fitting lid used for moist heat cookery such as braising.

Fajitas—A Mexican dish featuring meat that has been marinated in lime juice, oil and seasonings, then broiled or grilled and cut into strips. The strips are wrapped in warm flour tortillas with onions and bell peppers.

Feta Cheese—A classic Greek cheese, usually made from goat's milk, that is semi-soft and flaky, white in color with a salty, sharp flavor.

Fork Tender—Beef cooked until very tender; a fork can be inserted into the meat without resistance.

Garlic—A pungent seasoning of the same family as leeks, chives and onions. Flavor can range from mild to hot. The edible bulb or "head" grows underground; the bulb is made of sections called cloves. To peel garlic cloves, firmly press cloves with the flat side of a heavy knife to crack the skins. Chop or mince peeled garlic with a sharp knife, or crush it in a garlic press.

Gazpacho—A mixture of fresh tomatoes, bell peppers, onion, garlic, celery, cucumber, oil and vinegar, usually served as a cold soup.

Ginger—A spice that is both peppery and sweet in flavor and most often used in Oriental and Indian cookery. Available fresh as a knobby root, which must be peeled before use. Also available in powdered and crystallized forms.

Greek Olives—Assertively flavored purple-black ripe olives soaked in a wine-vinegar marinade and sold packed in either olive oil or vinegar. Also called Calamata or Kalamata olives.

Hoisin Sauce—A thick reddish-brown sauce made of soybeans, garlic, chili peppers and seasonings. Typically used in Chinese cookery as a condiment or flavoring for meat.

Jalapeño Pepper—Dark green, smooth skinned chili pepper with a flavor range from hot to very hot. Jalapeños are about 2 inches long and ¾ to 1 inch in diameter. The seeds and ribs are the hottest part of the pepper and can be removed, advisedly using hand protection, for a milder flavor.

Jicama—A large root vegetable often used in Mexican cookery. The white crunchy flesh has a sweet, nutty flavor and can be eaten raw or cooked. The thin brown skin should be peeled just before using.

Julienne—Food that has been cut into thin strips (about ⅛ inch thick).

Lentils—Seeds of the lentil legume used as a side dish (pureed, whole and/or combined with vegetables) and in salads, soups and stews.

Major Grey Chutney—A commercially available chutney made from mangoes.

Mango–A fruit originating in India. When ripe it has yellow skin mottled with red and a juicy, golden orange flesh that is both sweet and tart. A large flat seed runs lengthwise in the fruit; the fruit must be cut away from the seed with a sharp knife. Now grown in warm climates such as Mexico, California and Florida, mangoes are often used in Mexican and Caribbean cuisines.

Marinade–A seasoned mixture in which foods are marinated.

Marinate–To soak meat in a seasoned liquid mixture to add flavor and/or tenderize. Vegetables may also be marinated for flavor. Dry rubs are a type of flavor marinade.

Moo Shu–A stir-fried Chinese dish of short, thin strips of meat, vegetables, green onions and seasonings. The cooked meat mixture is rolled up in thin pancakes and served warm.

Mostaccioli–Tube shaped pasta about 2 inches long with diagonally cut ends. The surface can be ridged or smooth.

Mostacciollini–Thin mostaccioli. Also called penne.

Mustard (coarse-grain)–Prepared mustard containing mustard seeds.

Mustard (Dijon-style)–A pale yellow-gray prepared mustard with a sharp, hot flavor.

Penne–Thin tube shaped pasta with diagonally cut ends.

Picadillo–A dish of Spanish origin made of ground beef, tomatoes, garlic, onion and raisins often served over rice or used as a stuffing.

Picante Sauce–An uncooked spicy Mexican sauce made primarily with tomatoes, tomato sauce and hot peppers. Picante sauce and salsa are often used interchangeably in recipes. (*Picante* is Spanish for spicy.)

Pilaf–Rice cooked in stock or broth with various seasonings. Can contain other ingredients such as vegetables and meats. Served as a side or main dish. Pilaf is also made with other grains such as barley and bulgur (wheat kernels).

Piperade–A side or main dish made with a base of tomatoes and green bell peppers cooked in olive oil. Inspired by the Basque region of France.

Pita Bread–A Middle Eastern flat bread. When split horizontally, some pita breads form a pocket. Pita bread is sometimes called "pocket bread."

Plum Tomato–A small egg-shaped tomato available in red and yellow varieties; also called Italian plum tomatoes or Roma tomatoes.

Polenta–Italian cornmeal-based cooked cereal, or mush, eaten hot. Also, polenta can be chilled until firm, cut into pieces and sautéed, broiled or grilled.

Ratatouille–A dish from the Provence region of France made of eggplant, tomatoes, onions, bell pepper, zucchini, garlic and herbs cooked in olive oil and served hot or cold. Vegetables can vary depending upon availability.

Reduce–To decrease the amount and intensify the flavor of a liquid by boiling it rapidly in an uncovered pan.

Rice Vinegar–A mild Oriental vinegar made from fermented rice; sometimes called rice wine vinegar. Available in three types: white (clear or pale amber), red and black. White is most widely available.

Roasted Red Pepper–Red bell pepper that is cooked at high temperatures until the skin is blackened. After the pepper has cooled, the skin is removed. The flesh is soft, not crisp like a fresh pepper. Also available jarred; peppers must be rinsed and drained prior to using.

Salsa–Mexican term for "sauce." Salsa, an uncooked sauce of tomatoes, tomato sauce and hot peppers, is similar to Picante Sauce.

Satay–An Indonesian dish of marinated meat threaded onto skewers and grilled or broiled. Often served with a spicy peanut sauce.

Serrano Pepper–Small and tapering chili pepper about 1½ inches long with smooth, dark green skin that turns to orange and then yellow as it matures. Hotter than a jalapeño pepper.

Sesame Oil (dark)–A strongly flavored oil expressed from roasted sesame seeds, used as a flavor accent for Oriental dishes.

Shiitake–A type of mushroom originally from Japan and Korea with meaty flesh and a full flavor. Available fresh and dried.

Shredding (beef)–Beef that has been cooked to a very tender stage and can be pulled apart into thin strands using two forks.

Teriyaki–A sauce, often used in Japanese cookery, that consists of soy sauce, sake, sugar, ginger and seasonings.

Toasted (nuts and seeds)–Nuts or seeds that have been cooked in the oven, stove top or microwave oven for a short time until lightly browned. Toasting enhances the flavor.

Vermicelli–Pasta shaped in very thin strands, much thinner than spaghetti.

INDEX